LINCOLN CHRISTIAN COLLEGE AND SEMINARY

Games That Teach

. . . .

EXPERIENTIAL ACTIVITIES FOR REINFORCING LEARNING

Games That Teach

EXPERIENTIAL ACTIVITIES FOR REINFORCING LEARNING

STEVE SUGAR

Foreword by
SIVASAILAM "THIAGI" THIAGARAJAN

Jossey-Bass
Pfeiffer

San Francisco

ISBN:0–7879–4018–6

Library of Congress Catalog Card Number 97–076317

Printed in the United States of America

Published by

 350 Sansome Street, 5th Floor
San Francisco, California 94104–1342
(415) 433–1740; Fax (415) 433–0499
(800) 274–4434; Fax (800) 569–0443

Visit our website at: www.pfeiffer.com

Outside of the United States, Jossey-Bass/Pfeiffer products can be purchased from the following Simon & Schuster International Offices:

Simon & Schuster (Asia) Pte Ltd
317 Alexandra Road
#04–01 IKEA Building
Singapore 159965
Asia
65 476 4688; Fax 65 378 0370

Prentice Hall
Campus 400
Maylands Avenue
Hemel Hempstead
Hertfordshire HP2 7EZ
United Kingdom
44(0) 1442 881891; Fax 44(0) 1442 882288

Jossey-Bass/Pfeiffer
3255 Wyandotte Street East
Windsor, Ontario N8Y 1E9
Canada
888 866 5559; Fax 800 605 2665

Prentice Hall Professional
Locked Bag 507
Frenchs Forest PO NSW 2086
Australia
61 2 9454 2200; Fax 61 2 9453 0089

Prentice Hall/Pfeiffer
P.O. Box 1636
Randburg 2125
South Africa
27 11 781 0780; Fax 27 11 781 0781

Acquiring Editor: Matthew Holt
Director of Development: Kathleen Dolan Davies
Developmental Editor: Marian Prokop
Senior Production Editor: Dawn Kilgore
Interior Design & Illustrations: Gene Crofts
Cover Design: Brenda Duke

Printing 10 9 8 7 6 5 4 3 2

 This book is printed on acid-free, recycled stock that meets or exceeds the minimum GPO and EPA requirements for recycled paper.

To my mother

who always said I would never grow up.

I am so happy that you were so, so right.

Your loving Peter Pan.

Thanks

· ·

As with any endeavor, I want to thank some special friends who encouraged, prodded, and nagged me to publish this collection of games.

This list begins, and ends, with my wife and friend, Marie. She has always supported my writings and teachings—even when it meant travel to out-of-state conferences and classrooms.

And thanks to . . .

Thiagi, my model as a writer, teacher, and resource sharer. I have benefitted in borrowing from his ideas and writings and am proud that he has returned the favor.

George Takacs, who always listened and counseled me about problems in designs of games and lessons.

Dr. Karen Lawson, an ASTD colleague who supported my pursuits in writing and publishing.

Dr. Bob Preziosi, another ASTD colleague, who has supported my writings since our first meeting.

Carol Willett, a creative consultant for several games and writings.

Dr. Angus Reynolds, who brought my games to the graduate college curriculum.

Contents

. . . .

Part One

● CONFESSIONS OF A GAMES WRITER ●

Part Two

● 26 FRAME GAMES ●

Part Three

● INDEX ●

Credits

● ●

I would like to acknowledge colleagues who provided ideas and help with the following games:

- Beyond Tic-Tac-Toe: Dr. Sivasailam Thiagarajan (Thiagi)

- Bumper Stickers: George Takacs

- Conversations: Dr. Barbara Millis

- Deadlines: Dr. Robert Preziosi

- Hoops: Dr. SivasailamThiagarajan (Thiagi)

Foreword

● ●

In an informal survey that I did 20 years ago, only one trainer in 50 had used training games. Today, it is more likely that only one trainer in 50 has *not* used training games.

It is no longer necessary to justify or apologize for the use of training games. Participants and training managers demand the use of interactive experiential strategies. Training games are among the most popular tools in the trainer's kit; collections of training games outsell other types of how-to books for trainers. Training games are the method of choice among the new generation of participants brought up on *Sesame Street, MTV,* and *Nintendo®*. The focus on organizational learning emphasizes the importance of interactive training. The accent on teams demands techniques for collaborative learning. Field studies on accelerative learning and laboratory research on cognitive sciences have established the importance of different components of training games: active participation, diverse inputs, continuous interaction, rapid reinforcement, integrative review, and immediate application.

Games That Teach is an important addition to the growing number of books in this area. It is a unique collection of games that focus on reviewing and reinforcing what the participants have learned through other approaches. The games in this collection enable the trainers to combine the control and efficiency of conventional training with the interest and involvement of games.

In a recent informal poll, trainers and trainees identified the top three criteria for effective training games:

- The first of these criteria is *relevance*. Trainers and trainees demand a direct link between the training content and the play of the game. The games in this collection clearly meet this criterion. They are all framegames that can easily accommodate your specific content. Instructions in an early chapter show you how to create review questions and load the game templates. From this perspective, this is not a collection of a mere 26 games. It is a collection of 26 shells for producing hundreds of games.

- The second criterion for an effective training game is *flexibility*. You are in big trouble if your training game requires exactly 23 players, 47 minutes, and 80 poker chips. To be effective, a training game must accommodate different numbers of participants, time slots, and types of objectives. Each game in the collection comes with a set of suggestions on how to customize the activity to fit your needs.

- The third criterion for an effective training game is the *"freight-to-bait" ratio.* An effective training game should achieve an optimum balance between chance and skill. Too much chance renders the game boring and mindless. Too much emphasis on knowledge and skill reduces the game to an anxiety-provoking test. The games in this collection blend the appropriate amounts of fun and seriousness.

I have known Steve Sugar, the author, for 20 years and have seen him captivating skeptical participants in his ASTD and ISPI sessions with the games in this collection. Having dinner with Steve is always a unique experience. We don't waste our time with social banter or meaningful conversation. We just order our food, ask for extra napkins, pull out our pencils, and try to outsmart each other with our latest game creations. Steve is one of the best game designers in the training business. His playful spirit keeps cranking out creative games.

Here's a condensed summary of my reaction to *Games That Teach*: This is a collection of training games that I like. More importantly, this is a collection that I can use immediately.

I am sure that you will feel the same way about this book.

Sivasailam "Thiagi" Thiagarajan

March 1998

Preface

● ●

This is how learning is meant to be–active, passionate, and personal.

—Warren Bennis, *On Becoming a Leader*, p.89

From personal experience, I found that games can teach. It began in college, where I dabbled in a dry economics curriculum. My problem was how to avoid endless distractions and motivate myself into the required readings. During prolonged study periods, I began using playful mechanisms such as competing against the clock to complete a page or chapter. Building on this successful theme, I began to capture learning in the form of headlines or song titles. These mechanisms provided a way to interact with the material. And, once undertaken, the inertia of familiarity with the material ignited a modest passion for the topic. Ever-present deadlines then prodded me to complete the assignment.

● THE CHALLENGE

In the early 1970s, I was a guest at a New York Yankees baseball game. My host, an avid Yankee fan, issued the challenge—an even five-dollar bet that the Yankee outfielder, Bobby Mercer, would get three hits. The odds for any baseball player getting three hits in any game is remote, even in the middle of a winning batting spell. I took the bet, then settled in to document my winnings. But, Mercer quickly got two hits and was seeking his third as he approached home plate in the bottom of the eighth inning. Mercer worked to a full count of three balls and two strikes, then flied out to the leftfielder. I had won the bet. As I collected the five dollars, I asked my host why he had made such a fool's bet. His answer was simple: to make the game more interesting. And, it worked. I was absorbed in a dull game over the tenure of this modest bet.

Moving forward twenty-five years, I have found that these two factors—play and challenge—are fundamental to creating a successful game. Every game that has been successful must capture or intrigue the audience and then keep them involved. And, when properly translated, being mindful of the learning outcomes and audience, almost any classroom topic could be adapted to a learning game.

Features of Effective Games

Every game has its own format, a pattern of play and rules. A good game will have a subtle balance of fun (game play) and skill (content questions) that provide a dynamic learning environment. Features of good games include the following:

- User friendly: a game format that is easily explained and quickly understood.

- Easily adaptable: the game accepts your content, can be scaled up or down to any audience, and can be made more or else competitive, depending on the audience.

- Fun to play: the game evokes a "smile quotient" among the players.

- Challenging: the game keeps the players' interest throughout the contest.

- Portable: the game can be taken into any training site.

● REINFORCING LEARNING

In my years of sharing games with other training professionals, I have asked my audiences, "Why do you use games?" The overwhelming response has been "to reinforce topic material from lecture or readings." Although there are many other uses for games, this was my main theme for the games presented in this book. And, true to this theme, I offer twenty-six designs that review and reinforce material already covered.

The book is devoted to the play of games for your classroom and your learners. I urge you to review the seven-step game implementation model, and then browse through the designs. May your game experiences be positive, and your audiences enthusiastic!

● PART ONE ●

....

Confessions
of a Games Writer

....

A Note to the Trainer

• •

Today's learners demand more than the old lecture-and-learn formula. They want to interact and to become more personally involved with the lesson material. They want this involvement not in trivial or artificial ways, but in thoughtful exercises that evoke meaningful dialogue. This book approaches this requirement with twenty-six interactive games and exercises. Trainers can select from a palette of games, ranging from simple competitive exercises to in-depth challenges.

As a traveling teacher and writer of games, I have found that many presenters harbor anxieties about adapting and using games for their classrooms. This book will help you become an instant game designer in two ways:

- by presenting a seven-step game implementation model that walks you through each process of the game, from initial selection and adaptation to set-up and play and debrief, and

- by providing a template of each game that outlines its uses, sample play, and materials and supplies needed for its preparation and play.

By selecting a template and following the game model, I am certain that you will find uses for these games that go beyond anything this poor author envisioned during their design.

What Is a Frame Game?

••

*A learning game is a contrived framework through which
you present images of reality.*

The best example I can offer of a frame game is Tic-Tac-Toe. I have always enjoyed the reference to Tic-Tac-Toe as the world's oldest board game. I have never met anyone who has not played the game that has even been found etched onto the great pyramids of Egypt.

The beauty of the game format is that while it is simple to understand and play, it allows for many variations in content and uses. It is that "open frame" to which gamers allude. It accepts any material, can be adapted to any level of use, and is instantly recognizable. Although the game can be understood and played by children, I have seen it adapted for two popular television game shows in the United States—Tic-Tac-Dough and Hollywood Squares. Variations of the theme of this game can be found in countless models, including the expanding of the three-in-a-row requirement to the equally well-known Bingo format.

I have found yet another use for this reliable frame game. Using this game as my model, I can easily introduce the sometimes vaguely understood concept of how to use the game as a powerful learning tool by adapting it with customized material and focusing the performance objectives to a specific audience. It never fails. Because everyone is familiar with the game format, we can focus on the many uses, modifications, and techniques involved in adapting a game.

Tic-Tac-Toe can also stand the test of how to customize your own board game. To demonstrate this, I devoted a chapter on how to adapt this format into a board game for *The ASTD Handbook of Instructional Technology*. The chapter discussed production and adaptation techniques such as developing question cards, modifying the rules, and focusing on specific audiences.

If anyone wanted an instantly playable, patently user-friendly, adaptable board game, this would be my choice. The rules would be the same except that players could only cover spaces by appropriately answering questions (two for the center space). Questions could be given from question cards or from a central source, such as the instructor. You will find that by using Tic-Tac-Toe, or, to be more precise, the Tic-Tac-Two model, you will have a higher probability for a ready-made success. Then, as you grow in board game sophistication, you may wish to use other board game models.

The Seven-Step
Game Implementation Model

• •

This model is designed to assist you in customizing any game with your own material. Use the model as a guide, a reminder of the steps you must consider in the set-up, play, and debrief of your chosen game. After conducting each game, take notes on what worked well and what needed improvement; this information will guide your next use of that game.

Remember, these are your games, and they need your customizing in both content and implementation to meet the specific needs of your audience.

● STEP 1: GAME SELECTION

The following information should be considered in selecting the game for your learners.

Target Audience

One of the most important considerations is your target audience. Your game must reflect their knowledge, skills, abilities, and work environments. By simulating the "total working climate" of the player, you enhance the take-home value or application of the learning into the work site.

Games can evoke powerful learning. This begins when the learner, now a player, is challenged with the information item that provokes a search for the answer. When the correct answer is aired, the learning is immediately reinforced. This learning transfer happens over and over during the game. This "moment of learning" is not only powerful but often remains long after the learning event or game has been completed.

Knowing your audience affects the following aspects of games:

Level of Play. You may find that higher-level learners expect more from the game experience, especially in terms of the professionalism of the set-up and play and in the quality of the overhead transparencies, graphics, and accessories. In addition, this expectation impacts on the intellectual level of the content material provided in the lecture, handout materials, and in the questions and cases prepared for the game.

Number of Players. When games are involved, any number can play. Although many games seem best suited for smaller numbers of players, the intrigue and challenge of play can open learning to larger audiences. The key is the attraction to the play of the game that brings learners into active contact with the content or topic.

Most games are designed for smaller groups, usually two to sixteen players. Game play in smaller groups allows for more interaction between players, players and the material, and players and the facilitator. Adaptation for larger audiences usually requires the set-up and play of multiple game sets. Thus, a game that accommodates six players could be run in ten sets for a group of sixty. The trick is to devote additional time up front to organize game materials and ensure appropriate room layout.

The facilitator exerts more or less control, depending on audience size. The energies and distractions of larger groups require more maintenance and direct control. For larger audiences, the facilitator may wish to not only introduce game play but directly control all questions, supply correct answers and elaboration, and provide continuous game services, such as scoring and awarding of prizes. Audiences larger than twenty-five usually require the aid of a co-facilitator or assistant. Or, the facilitator may delegate some of the duties of distributing materials, posting scores, or collecting game sheets to members of the group.

Learning Outcomes

Know what you want your audience to learn or demonstrate during and after playing the game. Reinforcement games are excellent vehicles for learners to demonstrate the following, all within the friendly but competitive game environment:

- understanding of topic material from lecture and readings

- application of concepts and principles

- problem solving and strategizing

Playing Time

Time of play is always a critical issue. Because games are part of the total learning session, most facilitators prefer games that can be set-up, conducted, and debriefed in less than fifty minutes. This requires easily understood rules of play and an organized game experience.

Game play is only one part of the total game experience, which comprises three portions: set-up, play, and debrief.

1. Set-up (25 percent). This portion establishes the game environment by setting up the room, distributing game materials, dividing learners into teams, and reviewing the rules of play.

2. Play (50 percent). This is the actual play of the game, including start and stop of game play, clarifying questions about rules or content, and closure, such as declaring winners.

3. Debrief (25 percent). This portion processes game content and player conduct. To many facilitators, this is why they conduct a game: to have meaningful experiences, both learning and behavioral, that can be translated into insights and then applications for the work site.

Most of the games in this book are designed to be played in fifty minutes or less. Of course, if any game generates a highly motivating environment, you may extend the time of play by conducting additional rounds or by adding supplemental questions or tasks. Many facilitators feel that increased involvement equates to accelerated learning impact and increased take-home value of the experience.

Game Variations

Once you have selected and played the game, you may want to change the game format to meet your classroom needs. For example, you may want to change one of the following:

- Group size: accommodate smaller or larger groups.

- Time of play: expand or contract the total time allowed for the entire game, depending on the number of rounds, questions, or material you wish to cover in the time allowed.

- Focus of the task: adjust the levels of competition and cooperation, or encourage teamwork or creativity, etc.

- Scoring procedure: revise rewards and penalties as necessary.

In each of the games provided in this book, suggestions are listed for ways to adjust these four elements. Every trainer will have his or her own ideas for variations, but the ideas listed offer a starting point for modifying a game to suit a particular situation.

● STEP 2: GAME CONTENT: RESEARCH AND DEVELOPMENT

Desired Outcomes

Review your learning outcomes. What do you want the participants to learn from the game? These games are best suited for the review of information by recounting specific data and the identification of required items.

"Loading," or placing your content into the game, is a threefold process:

1. Select suitable information items for the game.

2. Translate these items into game-sized pieces or information nuggets by using short questions, mini case studies, or situations (for example, "demonstrate two low-cost, positive ways to deal with customers at the point of sale.")

3. Incorporate questions into the game format.

The following loading techniques were the most helpful in selecting and translating material into the game format. They can be used individually, or in a mix, to develop your game.

Technique #1. Final Exam. Develop a fifty-item post-class test to translate the most important concepts and facts into the game format. Go through the items and create an order for the game by prioritizing the items, creating a conceptual flow to the order of the questions, or using a random sequence.

Technique #2. Triage. Highlight important items and facts from your lesson material. Sort the material into "keep" and "drop" categories. Repeat the process until you have fifty items.

Technique #3. Story Board. Place significant items from your lesson material on 3" x 5" index cards. Categorize the cards by theme or concept. Then create a logical flow to the items for game use. The material from the cards can be edited into questions for the game.

Technique #4. Zoom In/Zoom Out. Remove yourself or "zoom out" from your material to gain a holistic overview. Then zoom in on specific incidents or questions that illustrate your learning points. Generate a tapestry of learning items that reinforce and assess participants' understanding of learning concepts.

Technique #5. Interview the SME. Interview a subject-matter expert (SME). Ask your expert about the most important learning aspects of the topic, what participants should know when they leave the class, underlying themes, and so on. Construct a pattern of questions that underscore the desired learning outcome.

Writing Questions

Appropriately written questions add to both the learning and fun of the game. Old tests are helpful, as well as the test banks that accompany classroom texts. Asking participants to develop questions adds to the question bank, provides fresh perspectives of the material, and even assists the learner in gaining a better understanding of the topic.

Following are some question-writing tips:

1. Write questions in a conversational format. Because game questions are usually read aloud, this helps the flow of the game.

2. Write closed-ended questions—questions requiring only one response. This ensures that the requested information and its rationale are covered in the question-and-answer format.

3. Focus each question on one fact. This keeps the information precise and brief. If needed, use several questions to ensure that the learning concept is covered adequately.

4. Be brief. Use simple wording for both questions and answers. Questions should contain thirty-five words or less and require only a brief statement as an answer. Brevity keeps the content portion from being a drawn-out question-and-answer process.

5. Develop a review-to-preview question mix. Write three review questions for every preview question. This will create a good question mix and pique interest in new topics. Even if the question material is new to the audience, it can be considered part of the randomness of play.

6. Mix the difficulty. Players become discouraged if they miss more than half of the questions, so try for an answer rate of 50 percent by creating a question difficulty mix of 1:3:1(that is, one challenging question, three moderate questions, and one easy question). Start with the easy and moderate questions to help learners get into the game. This allows new players to feel comfortable with both the game play and the content before they are challenged by more demanding questions.

7. Include the rationale or elaboration with the answers. This is a "moment of learning" when players are open to additional learning.

8. Number each question. This helps your question count and gives you a way to quickly identify questions that may require adjustment or updating.

Following are some proven question formats:

Direct question. This question requires players to identify a person, place, or thing. Be sure to include enough information to allow players to provide the proper answer.

Q: What one behavior has more impact on customer service than any other factor?

A. Cooperative behavior. Customers are more satisfied if they sense you are trying to help them.

Fill-in-the-blank. This requires the player to identify the information required by the blank space. Be careful to specify what is expected in the blank space.

Q: Five hundred studies document that ⎯⎯⎯⎯⎯ behavior had more impact on customer service than any other factor.

A: Cooperative

Multiple choice. This format presents the appropriate answer along with two distracting answers. This format can make difficult items easier by presenting a choice to the player. Questions for game play should aim at three choices. Avoid questions with four or more choices; they can be confusing and slow down play.

Q: Five hundred studies document that this one behavior had more impact on customer service than any other factor:

a. cooperative behavior

b. product knowledge

c. company loyalty

A: (a) cooperative behavior. Customers are more satisfied if they sense you are trying to help them. They expect you to know your product and be loyal to your company. What they are looking for is someone who pays attention to their needs.

True-false. This is the easiest question to prepare and answer, and it offers players a 50/50 chance to answer correctly. This question format can help players to ease into competition. Limit these questions to fewer than one in four to keep the game from becoming a "flip of the coin" match.

Q: Five hundred studies document that cooperative behavior had more impact on customer service than any other factor. True or False?

A: True.

Partial listing. This requires the multiple identification of items from a list. Ask for some, but not all, of the items. This "partial" format underscores the precedence without frustrating players in their attempts to recall the entire listing. The total list should be read when the answer is given.

Q: Name four of the seven behaviors that have a positive impact on customer service.

A: Accept any four of the following: cooperative behavior, product knowledge, sincerity, listening and/or asking questions, flexibility, patience, letting the customer know that you care

Lecture Material

Develop appropriate lecture materials to elaborate your questions or provide between-round and end-game commentary. This includes carefully prepared supplemental materials.

Games often enhance learner interest. Prepare a handout that is more than just "take-home" information from the presentation, containing ideas, applications, readings, resource lists, bibliography, etc., that underscore the entire learning experience. The handout may range from a thoughtful expansion of the question material to an in-depth reference manual. Handouts are traditionally distributed during class, but consider disseminating them prior to class to encourage pre-class study. Game play will reward those learners who took the time to go through the material.

Multimedia can add to the total learning experience. Consider other media, such as video dramatizations/case studies found in films (popular and training), audio dialogue or recordings, in-class demonstrations and models (laboratory samples), or computer simulations. (In all cases, remember to respect copyright laws.)

● STEP 3: GAME ACCESSORIES

Game accessories are materials that help create an appropriate game learning environment. You may want to invest in additional game accessories and props. Here is a starter list of equipment, materials, and props, with hints on how they may be used during the game:

Audiovisual Equipment

- Flip chart: Used to reinforce lecture, display game objective and rules of play, keep score, or list key elements of discussion.

  Using the flip chart to "bullet" or "headline" record the key elements of discussion has four major benefits. First, flip charting keeps key issues right in front of the group and helps them stay focused. Second, flip charts let the group cross-reference learning between different situations and helps prevent backtracking and needless repetition of the same issues and ideas. Third, a shared "record" reinforces the notion that learning is a group activity. This can reduce the tendency of some players to face off against one another in defense of their interpretations of events. Fourth, ideas recorded on the flip chart can be used to create new situations.

  Guidelines for being a recorder or scribe: Be neutral (capture everyone's points and do not edit). Use key words only; do not try to record comments verbatim. Invite corrections and ask for validation that you have captured the discussion points accurately. Write fast and legibly, using letters at least 1½" or 4 centimeters high.

- Overhead projector: Used to reinforce lecture, display game board, game objectives, and rules of play, keep score, and list comments and reactions. This is especially helpful for large groups.

- Audiotape player: Used to play background music to create a learning environment and to introduce audio information from speeches or sound tracks.

Game Materials and Accessories

- Felt-tipped markers: Used by both facilitator and learners for a variety of tasks from filling out name cards to listing responses on a flip chart.

- Masking tape: Used to place charts on walls, mend paper items, secure electrical wires, and so on.

- Game sheets: Used as playing surfaces, score sheets, or to present questions during game play.

Special Props

- Timer: Used to time rounds, question periods, debriefing or entire game period. A simple stopwatch or desk timer will work well.

- Noisemaker: Used to alert teams to start, stop, return from break, and so on. A whistle or chimes are playful ways to keep time.

- Name cards: Used to allow players to network and teams to create their own identities, promoting esprit de corps.

- Dice: Used as motivator in many games, especially board games. A roll of the dice is random and adds to the game environment.

  Note: Have several extra dice available. If a player complains about the performance of a specific die, simply swap that die for one from your supply. This addresses the complaint and models your interest in fair play.

- In-box: Used as a nice way to simulate the work environment when delivering assignments, game sheets, and special instructions.

- Prizes: Used to stimulate the game environment. Current data suggests that awarding prizes is inversely proportional to audience enthusiasm—the greater the natural energy of the audience, the lesser the need for using prizes for motivation. However, once prizes are mentioned, you must proceed with their award. Otherwise, this will be viewed as withholding of a promised benefit.

- Question cards: Used to ask or dispense specific information during game play. Although the use of question cards is usually associated with board games, they can also be used in facilitator-controlled games where a question is directed at the whole class or team. You may find it helpful to sequentially number all question cards for purposes of easy retrieval and updating.

- Raffle tickets: Used for drawing prizes. Tickets can be found at most stationery or office supply stores. Have players sign one portion and drop it into a container. Conduct a random draw at prize time. Some facilitators require winners to be present at the time of the drawing to help bring participants back from break. This policy can be introduced to the audience before each draw by establishing a "contract." This is done by asking the audience members if they approve the strategy that only participants in attendance can receive a prize. Thus, when a winner is drawn, but not present, the facilitator can draw again until an attending winner is found. Obtaining confirmation of this policy neutralizes complaints from participants not present at the time of the drawing.

- Glass bowl or container: Used to hold coupons for the drawing for prizes. Participants who match drawn ticket stubs win the prize.

- Chips: Used with board games to show rewards or status of play. Chips can also be used to cover spaces on bingo or tic-tac-toe game boards.

- Pawns: Used to denote a player's position on game board. Pawns can consist of almost any object, ranging from coins to paper clips. Pawns can also be customized to match the topic. For a pharmaceutical game board, the designer created "pill bottle" pawns using clear plastic coin tubes filled with colored candies.

● STEP 4: PRE-GAME SET UP: THE GOLDEN TIME

This time is critical, for readying the classroom and yourself. Take this time to walk through your game as you set up your game environment. Take on the perspective of your learner as you enter the room. Is the room visually attractive; does it reflect the game experience?

Conduct a room inspection, checking wall outlets, lighting, ventilation, and so on. Set up your tables, chairs, and name cards. Place posters, banners, work sheets, or wall charts containing quotations or art work. Later, post rules of play and other materials.

The instructor's table is your resource area. Take time to organize it with the game sheets and accessories for easy access during game play.

Lay out additional handouts and reference materials, as required. Lay out score sheets for distribution before and during the games. Lay out accessories, such as whistle, timer, overhead transparencies, prizes, and markers, as required.

Take this time to ensure that the equipment is appropriate and prepared. This includes:

- Flip chart easel(s). Make sure they are stable, in repair, and have sufficient paper. Post any pre-prepared flip chart pages. Check for markers and masking tape.

- Overhead projector. Make sure it is operable, focused, has an electric cord sufficiently long and secured to floor, is placed in a workable stand, and has an extra bulb.

- Video/audiotape player. Make sure they are operable, have appropriate power source (either battery or electric cord/outlet), and that tapes are readied and cued.

- Tables. Take this time to place four to six chairs in clusters around tables to establish a decision-making atmosphere. Make sure tables and chairs are cleared, clean, and in proper repair.

● STEP 5: GAME PRELIMINARIES

These are the in-class procedures prior to actual game play that help create the structure and environment of the game. They include such steps as:

- Dividing the group into teams (as required).

- Seating each team at its own table.

- Having team members fill out name cards.

- Having teams select team names, as needed.

- Distributing game materials.

- Distributing score sheets, question or problem sheets, flip chart paper, and other game accessories and props, as necessary.

- Displaying game information and player instructions on overhead transparencies or a flip chart.

Following is an example of using the game "tic-tac-two":

Introduce the game to the participants. The introduction, along with an interesting classroom layout, should motivate your learners to play. Audiences reflect and take on the enthusiasm displayed by the facilitator into game play.

> "Good morning, I want to briefly go over the game tic-tac-two. The game objective is to cover three spaces in a row horizontally, vertically, or diagonally. The game is played in rounds. Each round consists of a team selecting a space on the game sheet, and being asked a question. If team answers correctly, it covers selected space, then play alternates to other team. There is one

exception: If a team selects the center space, it is asked two questions. Both questions must be answered correctly to cover the space. If team answers incorrectly, its turn is completed, and play immediately alternates to other team. The game is played until one team gets three spaces in a row. Note that if neither team covers three spaces, both teams count number of correct answers. The team with the most correct answers is the winner."

● STEP 6: GAME PLAY

The game begins and the facilitator reads first question. If only one game is being played, answering teams responds to facilitator. If more than one game is being played, the answering team responds to its opponent.

After the team's answer, the facilitator may want to elaborate on reasons why the selected response is the most appropriate. As with all training situations, expect periodic resistance, defensiveness, or conflict while managing the game. Remember that while the question may have designated right and wrong answers, there may be other circumstances or answers not considered when the question was written. In this case, the objective is not to simply impose any one opinion or approach, but to get the learners to sort out the assumptions and details and encourage them to think about the information or situation created by the question.

Playing teams take appropriate action, covering the space if correct or ending the turn if incorrect.

The game is played the same for all rounds. The first team covering three spaces in a row is declared the winner. (*Note*: If a team covers three in a row before the facilitator completes his or her agenda of questions, simply congratulate the winners and invite them to return to play with the rest of the class. This acknowledges their win but continues play, as required.)

● STEP 7: CLOSURE/DEBRIEFING

Successful games usually motivate players to reach for the game objective, to "win." If the game objective is reached, then it should be acknowledged and rewarded, as appropriate. Then, in the after-glow of the game, attention can be re-focused on the topic plus any problems of game play, such as the rules, time periods, and quality of questions or team play. In the event of very competitive play, remind players that the goal was not just to win or get the right answers, but to demonstrate a working understanding of the topic. Thus, all competitive feelings, if any, should stay in the room. Players, now participants, should want to transfer positive learning experiences from this game back to the workplace.

Debriefing is the process of helping people reflect on their experiences to develop meaningful learning. It usually takes place immediately after the game experience. Guided debriefing involves the facilitator initiating and moderating the discussion. The debriefing period can include venting, where learners let off steam; shared insights; generalizations about relationship of game and content to real life; transfer, discussion of application of generalizations to the workplace; and speculations related to the game experience. Most instructors have their own method of debriefing, but may wish to follow a debriefing process of What? So What? and Now What?

- What? What did you experience? How do you feel? What happened? Chronologically?

- So What? What learning happened? What critical incidents in the game, decision process, or learning lead to insights? What did you learn from the readings or lecture that might have helped? What one major idea or concept did you learn? What are things that this relates to or reminds you of?

- Now What? What applications can be made to real-life, workplace? How does this relate to real life? If the same thing happened again, what would you do? From your experiences here, what behaviors would you show at the next meeting or work situation? What if these case studies actually happened at work? What if different folks from your organization were present?

Teaching by game has the unique challenge of matching the personality of the game—its ability to bring dimensions of playfulness and energy—to the demands of the topic and audience. This means that no matter how many times you play the same game, even with the same material, audience reactions differ. Each audience has its own learning thresholds and perceptions of what is new and important. So, as you act as guide and facilitator, you get to experience the joy of discovery along with each audience.

To serve you, each game offers sample play along with recommended tips on customizing for your audience. This should help you select and adapt material for the critical first rounds of play. Then, as you feel more comfortable with the game, you can customize game play by varying the topics and rules.

Finally, these games can be used as either "stand-alone" activities—to introduce, teach, review, or test learning—or sequenced with other games or activities to create a mix of learning.

● PART TWO ●

. . . .

26 Frame Games

. . . .

Best Shot

....

● PURPOSE

- To allow participants the opportunity to "shoot" at a target, and then answer questions for points.

- To review topic material from lecture or readings.

● SUPPLIES

- An overhead transparency or newsprint flip chart page of the Player Instructions for Best Shot, prepared in advance by the facilitator.

- An overhead projector (if using transparencies).

- A newsprint flip chart and felt-tipped markers.

- A set of questions, prepared in advance by the facilitator.

- One laser pointer (or narrow-beam flashlight) for each team.

- One or more targets, prepared in advance with a designated bull's-eye area.

- Masking tape.

- Paper and pencils for the participants.

- A whistle or other noisemaker to initiate play.

● STEPS

1. Divide the group into two or three teams.

2. Post the prepared target on a flip chart or on the wall.

3. Set up a shooter's line on the floor with masking tape.

4. Define the task: "One player from each team aims and shoots a laser pointer at the target. The team whose player made the best shot—whose red dot or light is nearest to designated target—answers a question. If he or she answers correctly, that team receives 2 points. If the answer is incorrect, the team loses 2 points. If the answer is incorrect, the player with the next closest shot has the option to answer the question." (*Note:* Second player would also receive 2 points for a correct answer or lose 2 points for an incorrect answer.)

5. Display the Player Instructions. Round 1 begins, and the scores for each team are posted on a newsprint flip chart.

6. Play continues the same way for each round. At the end of play, the team with the most points is declared the winner.

● CUSTOMIZING BEST SHOT

Regarding Group Size

- Allow teams to consult with the player before answering the question. Especially with larger groups, this keeps everyone more involved.

Regarding Time

- Put time limits on how long a player can take to answer.

- Vary the number of rounds according to the time available.

Regarding the Focus of the Task

- Allow teams to consult on the answers to the questions.

- Use open-ended questions or analytical case studies.

Regarding Scoring

- Adjust the value of a correct answer by proximity to the bull's-eye. For example, hitting the bull's-eye is worth 5 points, the area next to the bull's-eye is worth 3 points, and the outer areas are worth 1 point.

- Allow players 5 seconds to place multiple shots in the target area. Each team is asked a question, and a correct answer scores points corresponding to the number of hits. An incorrect answer or no answer loses 5 points.

- Select a player from each team to shoot at the bull's-eye of the target. If the player hits the bull's-eye and provides the correct answer, the team scores 7 points. If the player hits the bull's-eye and provides an incorrect answer, the team scores 2 points. If the player misses the bull's-eye and provides the correct answer, the team scores 3 points. If the player misses the bull's-eye and provides an incorrect answer, the team scores 0 points.

Best Shot

- **Players shoot laser pointer beams at a target.**

- **The player with the shot closest to the target answers a question.**

- **If the answer is correct, that player's team receives 2 points.**

- **If the answer is incorrect, that player's team loses 2 points.**

- **The player with the next closest shot then has the option to answer that question.**

- **The team with the most points wins.**

Jossey-Bass/Pfeiffer

Beyond Tic-Tac-Toe

● PURPOSE

- To challenge teams to think within the box by answering questions about a topic.

- To challenge teams to think outside the box by creatively covering spaces on a game board.

- To warm up the group with a creativity exercise.

● SUPPLIES

- An overhead transparency or newsprint flip chart page of the Player Instructions for Beyond Tic-Tac-Toe, prepared in advance by the facilitator.

- An overhead projector (if using transparencies).

- A newsprint flip chart and felt-tipped markers.

- A set of questions, prepared in advance by the facilitator.

- One copy of the Game Sheet for Beyond Tic-Tac-Toe.

- Nine game pieces for each team. The game pieces for each team consist of three rectangles, three squares, and three triangles of the same color. Each shape should have a small, medium, and large version. The game pieces should be sized to fit the spaces on the game board.

● STEPS

1. Divide the group into two teams and give one set of game pieces to each team.

2. Define the task: "Each team in turn will be asked a question. If the team provides a correct answer, it uses one of its game pieces to cover a space on the game board. If the team provides an incorrect answer, play alternates to the other team. The object of the game is to complete a line of three spaces in a row, either horizontally, vertically, or diagonally."

3. Post the Player Instructions, and begin the game.

4. Play continues until time is called. Note that both teams are allowed to occupy the same space on the game board, although they have not been told this information directly. Inasmuch as part of the purpose of this game is "outside-the-box" thinking, this idea may have to be seeded to the participants.

5. At the end of the game, have each team tally how many lines it has with three game pieces in a row. The team with the most lines wins.

6. Debrief the activity, focusing on "outside-of-the-box" play.

● SCORING EXAMPLE

1. Team 1 is asked a question and provides the correct answer. Team 1 places a medium green triangle in center space. Play alternates to Team 2.

2. Team 2 is asked a question and provides the correct answer. Team 2 places a large red square in the upper-right corner space. Play alternates to Team 1.

3. Team 1 is asked a question and provides an incorrect answer. Play alternates to Team 2.

4. Team 2 is asked a question and provides the correct answer. Team 2 places a large red square in the upper-left corner space. Play alternates to Team 1.

5. Team 1 is asked a question and provides the correct answer. Team 1 places a medium green triangle in the upper-middle space. Play alternates to Team 2.

6. Team 2 is asked a question and provides the correct answer. Team 2 places a small red square in the upper-middle space, alongside the green triangle. Team 2 claims to have three red squares in a row. Team 1 disagrees, stating that it already occupied the space. The facilitator confirms Team 2's claim. Play alternates to Team 1.

7. Team 1 is asked a question and provides the correct answer. Team 1 places a medium green triangle in the lower-middle space. Team 1 claims three green triangles in a row. Play alternates to Team 2.

● CUSTOMIZING BEYOND TIC-TAC-TOE

Regarding Group Size

- Adjust the game to suit the size of the group by running several games simultaneously. This requires briefing one or more of the participants about the option of having more than one game piece on a space.

Regarding Time

- Set time limits for teams to answer their questions.

- Play for a specific length of time or for a specific number of rounds.

Regarding the Focus of the Task

- Allow a team to challenge the other team's answers.

- Have team members take turns answering the questions.

Regarding Scoring

- Vary the difficulty of the questions and allow teams to place more than one game piece on the board when they answer more difficult questions.

- Award bonus points based on "outside-of-the-box" thinking.

Beyond Tic-Tac-Toe

Jossey-Bass/Pfeiffer

Beyond Tic-Tac-Toe

. . . .

- **Each team answers a question.**

- **If the answer is correct, the team places a game piece on a space.**

- **Teams try to get 3 game pieces in a row.**

Bumper Stickers

• •

● PURPOSE

- To demonstrate participants' understanding or perspective of a topic.

- To develop the most memorable "bumper sticker" slogan.

● SUPPLIES

- An overhead transparency or newsprint flip chart page of the Player Instructions for Bumper Stickers, prepared in advance by the facilitator.

- An overhead projector (if using transparencies) or newsprint flip chart and felt-tipped markers.

- Large strips of paper, approximately 5" by 24". (*Note:* These strips may be cut from the pages of a newsprint flip chart.)

- Assorted colors of felt-tipped markers for the participants.

- Paper and pencils for each participant.

- Masking tape or thumbtacks for posting strips of paper.

- Prizes (optional).

● STEPS

1. Divide the group into teams of two to five players each.

2. Distribute paper, pencils, strips of paper, and felt-tipped markers to each team.

3. Define the task: "Take five minutes to write a slogan or bumper sticker that summarizes what you learned from this session."

4. Post the Player Instructions for Bumper Stickers, using an overhead transparency or newsprint flip chart.

5. After five minutes, call time and invite each team in turn to post its bumper sticker and present it to the rest of the group.

6. Debrief the participants about what the bumper stickers indicate about what they have learned about this topic.

7. (Optional.) Poll the participants about the best bumper sticker and award prizes to the winning team.

● CUSTOMIZING BUMPER STICKERS

Regarding Group Size

- Assign each individual to create his or her own bumper sticker if the group is small.

Regarding Time

- Allow teams to create a series of slogans or bumper stickers, as time allows.

Regarding the Focus of the Task

- Assign each team to summarize a selected portion of the session or the assigned reading with its bumper sticker.

- Assign the teams to create slogans or bumper stickers for a new product.

- Assign the teams to create slogans or bumper stickers that describe the company's mission statement.

Regarding Scoring

- Use this assignment at various times during a training session, allowing teams or individuals to accumulate points. Points may be assigned for originality, humor, accuracy, or any other appropriate consideration.

Bumper Stickers

- Create a slogan about the assigned topic (5 minutes).

- Make a bumper sticker.

- Post and explain your bumper sticker.

By the Numbers

. . . .

● PURPOSE

- To offer a lively method to review material, especially technical material.

● SUPPLIES

- An overhead transparency or newsprint flip chart page of the Player Instructions for By the Numbers, prepared in advance by the facilitator.

- An overhead projector (if using transparencies).

- A newsprint flip chart and felt-tipped markers.

- A set of questions, prepared in advance by the facilitator.

- One or more dice (one if used by the facilitator; one for each table if used by the participants).

- One name tent for each participant and assorted felt-tipped markers.

- Paper and pencils for the participants.

- A stopwatch or other timing device.

- A whistle or other noisemaking device.

1. Divide the group into teams of five to six players. Distribute name tents and felt-tipped markers to each team.

2. Define the task: "All players at your table are on the same team. Each player on your team is assigned a different number between one and six. Write your name and your assigned number on your name tent and put it in front of you. I will read a question, then roll a die and announce the number. The player whose number matches the roll of the die must answer the question. If he or she answers correctly, the team receives one point. If he or she answers incorrectly, the team is penalized one point. There is a 15-second time limit for answers."

3. Post the Player Instructions; begin the game by asking a question and then rolling a die to determine which players are eligible to answer. (*Note:* For teams of five, if the die shows a six, it will be re-thrown until a number of five or less is shown.) Allow 15 seconds for responses, then call time.

4. If a player has answered correctly within the 15-second time limit, award 1 point to that team. If a player has answered incorrectly, deduct 1 point from that team's score. Post the results on a newsprint sheet.

5. After a designated time period or number of rounds, the team with the most points is declared the winner.

● CUSTOMIZING BY THE NUMBERS

Regarding Group Size

• Form as many teams as necessary to accommodate larger groups.

Regarding Time

• Vary the time limit for answers.

• Conduct a specific number of rounds or play for a specified amount of time.

Regarding the Focus of the Task

• Have all non-answering players write down their answers. This keeps everyone involved during the question-and-answer process. If the designated player's answer is incorrect, another player's answer can be reported. If correct, the team will not be penalized a point, but will remain even for the round.

- Designate a time frame, announce a topic, and instruct each team to create as many answers as possible.

Regarding Scoring

- Have each team roll its own die to determine which player will answer the question.

- Base the point values of individual questions on their difficulty.

By the Numbers

• **Assign each player a number between one and six.**

• **The facilitator rolls a die.**

• **The players whose numbers match the roll must answer the question within 15 seconds.**

• **If the answer is correct, the team receives 1 point.**

• **If the answer is incorrect, the team loses 1 point.**

Classify

• •

● PURPOSE

- To offer participants the opportunity to classify items correctly.

- To demonstrate differences among similar items or processes.

● SUPPLIES

- An overhead transparency or newsprint flip chart page of the Player Instructions for Classify, prepared in advance by the facilitator.

- An overhead projector (if using transparencies).

- Two or more newsprint flip chart pages, prepared in advance by the facilitator with the names of the categories to be used in the activity.

- A newsprint flip chart and assorted felt-tipped markers.

- A set of items or processes for each team, written on 3" x 5" index cards, prepared in advance by the facilitator.

- Masking tape.

- A stopwatch or other timing device.

● STEPS

1. Divide the group into two teams of five to ten players each. Post the two prepared sheets of newsprint that list the categories to be used in the activity, as well as the Player Instructions.

2. Define the task: "You will receive a set of statements that refer to one of two or more processes. The player from Team A will have one minute to sort the statements into the proper categories. Each statement must be categorized before the next statement can be read, and the team may not help its player. At the end of one minute, Team A will receive 1 point for each item correctly sorted, but 0 points for each incorrectly sorted item. Then play will resume with Team B."

3. The first player stands at the posted category sheets. He or she turns over the first card, decides where it belongs, and uses masking tape to attach it to the category sheet. The player must attach the first card to the category sheet before reading the next card.

4. Call time at the end of 1 minute. Award 1 point to Team A for each correctly categorized statement. Reposition any incorrectly placed statements, and set up for the next round.

5. Each round is played in the same manner, and scores are cumulative for each team. Once all of the statements have been categorized, the team with the most points is declared the winner.

In a round of time management, players must place the items in the most appropriate category. The headings "time saver," "time waster," and "both" are placed on the board and ten index cards are placed face down on the table. The player from the first team must correctly place as many cards as possible under the correct headings in 60 seconds. Each correct placement earns 1 point; each incorrect placement receives 0 points. Remember, once a card is selected, it *must* be placed in one of the categories. The player makes the following choices:

	Time Saver	Time Waster	Both	Score
Meetings		✓		+1
Telephone			✓	+1
"To do" list	✓			+1
Interruptions		✓		+1
Using more than one scheduling calendar	✔̸	✗		0
Watching television		✓		+1
Crises management	✔̸	✗		0
Receiving agenda prior to meeting	✓			+1
Planning next work day evening before	✓			+1
Having time-saving devices such as e-mail and fax			✓	+1
Total points				+8

Legend: ✓ = correct answer
             ✔̸ = incorrect answer
             ✗ = corrected answer

● CUSTOMIZING CLASSIFY

Regarding Group Size

- Conduct more than one game simultaneously by supplying answer keys to participants who are designated to observe. These participants time the rounds and rule on how the statements have been categorized.

Regarding Time

- Allow more time in each round for more difficult sets of questions, and less time for less difficult sets of questions.

Regarding the Focus of the Task

- Allow teams to coach their players as they are making their decisions.

- Allow teams to meet before each round to plan strategy and communication patterns.

- Have participants take short self-tests to preview their own attitudes or perceptions of the class discussion. The pretest should require only one or two minutes of time. This "gut" check allows participants to see and evaluate their own perceptions. Headings can be polar, reflecting both sides of the issue or topic, such as "proper" and "improper." Using a third choice, such as "undecided," allows participants to hedge. Using the heading "both" requires participants to view both sides of the issue.

- Expand the format to a "forced choice" for multiple headings, such as the four stages of team development. Require individual players, or teams, to place each card in the correct stage of team development.

Card Reads:	Team Stage
Members are anxious about and suspicious of the task ahead.	Forming
Some members demonstrate passive resistance.	Storming
Disagreements become more civilized and less divisive.	Norming
Team becomes creative in accomplishing its goal.	Performing

Regarding Scoring

- Change the scoring so that 1 point is deducted for incorrect answers in addition to the 1 point awarded for correct answers. This might be especially appropriate for rounds during which the team can coach the individual player.

Classify

....

- ## The first player begins.

- ## The player turns over the first card.

- ## The player categorizes the statement and attaches it to the appropriate list.

- ## The player turns over the next card.

- ## Play stops at the end of one minute.

- ## Team is awarded 1 point for each correct answer.

Conversations

● ●

● **PURPOSE**

- To offer participants the opportunity to respond to and complete mini-problem statements based on classroom topics.

- To create dialogue on a given set of topics.

● **SUPPLIES**

- An overhead transparency or newsprint flip chart page of the Player Instructions for Conversations, prepared in advance by the facilitator.

- An overhead projector (if using transparencies) or a newsprint flip chart and felt-tipped markers.

- A set of Game Sheets for Conversations, prepared in advance by the facilitator. (See samples provided at the end of this game.)

- One container or bowl for each game sheet assigned.

- One pair of scissors.

- A whistle or other noisemaking device.

● **STEPS**

1. Distribute a packet of two or more Game Sheets to each participant. (*Note:* All game sheets are identical.)

---

2. Define the task: "Sign the bottom of each game sheet. As directed by the instructions, work alone, in pairs, or in small groups. Complete each game sheet, cut off the bottom of the sheet, and deposit it in the appropriate container."

3. Designate the amount of time allotted for the activity, and post the Player Instructions.

4. At the end of the allotted time, reconvene the group. Draw one or more entries from each container, and invite the participants who submitted those entries to share their input with the group.

5. Encourage discussion, and debrief as needed.

● CUSTOMIZING CONVERSATIONS

Regarding Group Size

- Accommodate larger groups by including more small group activities in the set of game sheets, and by expanding from three to four members in the group.

Regarding Time

- Determine a time limit for the activity, and adjust the number of game sheets accordingly.

- Vary the time for the activity depending on the complexity of the assignments on the game sheets.

Regarding the Focus of the Task

- Adapt the activity to suit the particular needs and interests of your group.

- Encourage participants to get to know one another by including assignments that are highly interactive.

- Foster competition or cooperation, depending on the number of individual and the number of group tasks assigned on the game sheets.

Regarding Scoring

- Award points based on the number of game sheets each participant completed.

- Poll participants to vote for the most interesting or most original answers, and award prizes.

Conversations

- Sign the bottom of each game sheet.

- Complete each sheet as directed.

- Detach the bottom portion of the sheet and deposit it in the appropriate container.

Jossey-Bass/Pfeiffer

SAMPLE GAME SHEETS FOR
Conversations

. . . .

● **CONVERSATIONS GAME SHEET #1: REFERENCE BOOKS**

Instructions: This activity requires you to work alone. Think of the last time you purchased a book for your professional library. Then answer this inquiry: How do I select which books to read? When you have completed the top portion of this form, detach the bottom portion and place it in the appropriate glass bowl.

✂ -
Detach here

Game Sheet #1: Reference Books

Participant Name

● CONVERSATIONS GAME SHEET #2: MEETINGS

Instructions: Find a partner. As a team, develop two solutions for this problem: How to get colleagues to be punctual and prepared for meetings? When you have completed the top portion of this form, detach the bottom portion and place it in the appropriate glass bowl.

1.

2.

✂ Detach here

Game Sheet #2: Meetings

Participant Name

Partner's Name

● CONVERSATIONS GAME SHEET #3: COMPUTERS

Instructions: Form a group of three. As a team, find three approaches to this inquiry: How do I use computers to assist me in my job? When you have completed the top portion of this form, detach the bottom portion and place it in the appropriate glass bowl.

   1.

   2.

   3.

✂ Detach here

Game Sheet #3: Computers

   Participant Name

   Partner #2

   Partner #3

Deadlines

. . . .

● PURPOSE

- To predict how accurately a team can answer sets of questions pertaining to a certain topic.

- To collect points based on both the accuracy of the predictions and the accuracy of the answers.

● SUPPLIES

- An overhead transparency or newsprint flip chart page of the Player Instructions for Deadlines, prepared in advance by the facilitator.

- A newsprint flip chart page of the Scoring Matrix for Deadlines, prepared in advance by the facilitator.

- An overhead projector (if using transparencies).

- A newsprint flip chart and felt-tipped markers.

- One set of Question Sheets for Deadlines for each team, prepared in advance by the facilitator. (*Note:* Each Question Sheet consists of seven questions. Each round of play requires one Question Sheet. The number of Question Sheets prepared is at the discretion of the facilitator. A sample is provided at the end of this game.)

- Paper and pencils for each participant.

Deadlines

- **Estimate the number of questions you will answer correctly.**

- **Answer the questions.**

- **Compute your scores according to the Scoring Matrix.**

SCORING MATRIX FOR
Deadlines

··

Estimated Number of Correct Answers	Total Points
1	1
2	4
3	9
4	16
5	25
6	36
7	49

If a team does not accomplish its contract, it receives 2 points for each correct answer. If a team exceeds its contract, it receives an additional 2 points for every correct answer above the estimate.

SAMPLE QUESTION SHEET FOR
Deadlines

• •

Team #

We will answer _____ questions correctly.

Estimated number of points:

Actual points:

1. What is the most important feature of any filing system?

2. Who is more likely to make and follow a daily "to do" list—men or women?

3. Of time spent in meetings, approximately what percent do North Americans feel is wasted?

4. What is the standard size of paper crossing the American professional's desk?

5. Under normal conditions, what is the optimum number of people who should be involved in a decision?

6. What is the best time of day to plan your next work day?

7. According to support staff, what is their most frequently performed activity?

Answer Key (for the facilitator):

1. Being able to find or retrieve items quickly.

2. Women. Source: 21st Century Workplace Study by Priority Management

3. 50 percent (accept from 45 percent to 55 percent). Time wasters include unclear or no agenda, no resolution, not beginning promptly.

4. 8.5" x 11" (21 x 28 cm). This must be considered in plans for handling and storing of office papers.

5. Five (accept from four to six). Source: Executives at Motorola, a leader in team-based quality management.

6. The evening before. This gives you a clear picture of where you want to go and it gets you off to a "flying start" the next day.

7. Answering the telephone.

Deep Six

· ·

● **PURPOSE**

- To collect points by rolling a die and answering review questions from lectures or readings.

● **SUPPLIES**

- An overhead transparency or newsprint flip chart page of the Player Instructions for Deep Six, prepared in advance by the facilitator.

- An overhead projector (if using transparencies) or a newsprint flip chart and felt-tipped markers.

- A set of questions, prepared in advance by the facilitator.

- A copy of the Game Sheet for Deep Six for each team.

- One die per team.

- Paper and pencils for the participants.

● **STEPS**

1. Divide the group into teams of three to five players each. Distribute Game Sheets, dice, paper, and pencils.

2. Define the task: "The object is to collect as many points as you can. To score points you roll a die and answer questions. Scoring is based on the number

shown on the face of the die and providing the correct answer. Each team continues to roll until it rolls a six. At that point, the team must answer its last question—a correct answer earns 6 points, and an incorrect answer loses 6 points."

3. Display the Player Instructions, and begin play. The first team continues until it rolls a 6, at which point the second team begins its turn. Continue until all teams have had a turn.

4. Play additional rounds as time permits. The team with the most points at the end of play is declared the winner.

● SCORING EXAMPLE

1. Team A rolls a 5. The team provides the correct answer to the question. Team A records 5 points on line 1 of its game sheet.

2. Team A rolls a 3. The team provides an incorrect answer and records a 0 on line 2 of its game sheet. Team A's total now is 5 points.

3. Team A rolls a 4, then provides the correct answer to the question that is asked. Team A records a 4 on line 3 of to the game sheet, bringing its total to 9 points.

4. Team A rolls a 6, which signals its final roll this round. Team A provides a correct answer to the question; therefore, Team A records a 6 on line 4 of its game sheet, bringing its total to 15 points. (Note that if Team A had answered incorrectly, 6 points would have been deducted from its score, leaving 3 points.)

● CUSTOMIZING DEEP SIX

Regarding Group Size

• Conduct several games simultaneously with large groups. Divide the class into sets of two teams. The first team is given questions prepared by the facilitator and reads those questions to its opponent. When the answering team has completed its turn, it then reads the remaining facilitator questions to the first team. After both teams have completed their turns, total the scores. The team with the most points is declared the winner.

- Provide sets of questions and one die to each team. Designate one of the participants to observe and supply him or her with an answer key. Play the game in the same manner.

Regarding Time

- Set a time limit for a round of play, such as three minutes.

- Set time limits for teams to decide on their answers to questions.

Regarding the Focus of the Task

- Have each player in turn answer a question, rather than the team as a whole.

Regarding Scoring

- Allow teams to double the point value of the roll before hearing the question. If the answer is correct, the team receives twice the number of points; if the answer is incorrect, the team loses twice the number of points.

Deep Six

Team

Roll #	Die Roll	Correct Answer?	Score
Roll 1			
Roll 2			
Roll 3			
Roll 4			
Roll 5			
Roll 6			
Roll 7			
Roll 8			
Roll 9			
			Total Score

Deep Six

....

- Team A rolls a die and answers a question.

- If correct, Team A scores points corresponding to the number on the die.

- If incorrect, Team A scores 0 points.

- Team A continues to roll until it rolls a 6, which will be its last question for this round.

- If Team A answers that question correctly, it receives 6 points.

- If Team A answers incorrectly, it loses 6 points.

- Play passes to Team B.

- At the end of play, the team with the most points wins.

Find Points

●●

● **PURPOSE**

- To guide participants to find items from clues taken from readings or handout materials.

- To reinforce learning concepts found in handouts or readings.

● **SUPPLIES**

- An overhead transparency or newsprint flip chart page of the Player Instructions for Find Points, prepared in advance by the facilitator.

- An overhead projector (if using transparencies) or a newsprint flip chart and felt-tipped markers.

- A copy of the Work Sheet for Find Points, prepared in advance by the facilitator.

- Paper and pencils for the participants.

- Extra copies of handouts or reading material, as required.

● **STEPS**

1. Divide the group into teams of one to three players each. Distribute a copy of the work sheet to each team. Post the Player Instructions.

2. Define the task: "This work sheet contains learning points from your reading material. Next to each point is a clue to help you find the information in your reading material and to identify the item correctly. You have five minutes to complete the work sheet."

---

3. Call time at the end of five minutes. Have each team in turn read its response to the first item. Award one point for each clue solved.

4. Continue having teams read their responses to the remaining questions, awarding points in the same way.

5. Debrief the activity and discuss any questions that may have arisen.

6. Designate winners, as appropriate.

● CUSTOMIZING FIND POINTS

Regarding Group Size

- Create a variety of work sheets and distribute them at random so that the team reports do not get repetitive.

- Assign half of the group to write questions based on readings; the next session, assign the other half of the group to be the question writers.

Regarding Time

- Shorten the time required by assigning only one or two questions to each team.

- Lengthen the activity either by using more difficult questions or by increasing the number of questions to be answered.

- Designate the work sheet as a take-home assignment.

Regarding the Focus of the Task

- Use Find Points as a review of previous material or as a pretest of knowledge about upcoming material.

- Design separate questions and clues for each participant. Use the activity as a guided writing assignment about the key points of a specific topic. Have each participant present his or her assignment to the rest of the group.

- Have one or more participants prepare their own work sheets to be handed in or presented to the rest of the group. This assignment can give insights on what participants find important or interesting.

Regarding Scoring

- Award extra points based on how long the team took to complete the work sheet.

- Include bonus questions that are worth extra points.

PLAYER INSTRUCTIONS FOR
Find Points

- **Find information in your reading material, based on clues.**

- **When time is called, read your responses.**

- **The team earns 1 point for each correct answer.**

Find Points

Time Management Reading: Dealing with People Interruptions

Business professionals rate interruptions as the biggest time waster by a three-to-one margin. In some jobs, interruptions take up 50 percent to 70 percent of the day. Many interruptions are *people*—people who want you to shift your attention from what you're doing to something else. Here are some tips:

Short and Sweet. Make efforts to keep interruptions short. Set time limits at the beginning—"I can only give you five minutes. If that's not sufficient, we'll have to schedule a time later in the week. Okay?"

The "Regulars." If 80 percent of your interruptions are made by 20 percent of the people, these people are considered "regulars." Have them save up their items for one-on-one meetings.

"Time Window." Cut down on unannounced interruptions by scheduling time when you're available—"I'm always available for questions from 1:00 to 3:00 p.m."

Quiet Time. Alert others that you prefer not to be interrupted for the next one-half to one hour. This technique is also suited to entire offices.

Turn Your Desk to the Wall. Visual interruptions are more disruptive than auditory ones (by a four-to-one margin). Turning your desk away prevents eye contact with drop-in visitors.

Hard of Hearing. If it looks like you are going to be interrupted, teach yourself to keep working until you are at a spot where you can take a break. This will help you get more work done and discourage this interrupter in the future.

Get in Early. A famous United States senator used to get into the office at 5:00 a.m. to get his paperwork done before the phones began ringing at 9:00 a.m.

Refusal Skills. Realize that you have the right to say "no." Offer a counter proposal when you feel it is appropriate. Learn a script for refusing, such as "that sounds like a wonderful opportunity, but my own work schedule is enough for me right now."

Gauntlet

. . . .

● **PURPOSE**

- To acquaint participants with how strategic decisions affect the points earned for answering questions.

- To review topic material from lecture or readings.

- To encourage team analysis and play.

● **SUPPLIES**

- An overhead transparency or newsprint flip chart page of the Player Instructions for Gauntlet, prepared in advance by the facilitator.

- An overhead projector (if using transparencies) or a newsprint flip chart and felt-tipped markers.

- A set of questions, prepared in advance by the facilitator.

- One copy of the Game Sheet for Gauntlet per game.

- Two sets of dice per game, with two of one color and two of another color.

- Paper and pencils for the participants.

● **STEPS**

1. Divide the group into two teams of three to five players each, and give them one game sheet, one answer sheet, and two sets of dice.

2. Define the task: "The first team will roll two dice. That team can choose to cross off on the game sheet either the sum of the dice or the numbers shown on each die. Then the team answers a question. If the team answers correctly, it records the points in the appropriate columns on the game sheet. If the team answers incorrectly, the team records 0 points in the appropriate columns on the game sheet. Then play alternates to the other team. Play continues until one team cannot complete its turn (that is, cannot cross off either the sum of the two dice or both of the individual numbers on the game sheet). The team that makes the last complete dice roll receives bonus points."

3. Display the Player Instructions and begin play. Play continues until one team or the other cannot complete its turn. At that point, the team with the most points is declared the winner.

● SCORING EXAMPLE

1. Team A rolls a 4 and a 5. The team has the option of selecting either the 9 or the 4 and 5. Team A chooses to cross off the 4 and the 5. The team answers the question correctly and records 4 points on line 4 of the game sheet and 5 points on line 5 of the game sheet.

2. Play alternates to Team B, who rolls a 3 and a 4. Team B cannot cross off the 3 and 4 because the 4 has already been deleted. Team B still can delete the 7 from the game sheet, and does so. The team answers the question incorrectly and records 0 points on line 7 of the game sheet.

3. Play alternates to Team A. Team A rolls a 4 and a 5. The 4 and 5 are already taken, so Team A deletes 9 from the game sheet. The team answers the question correctly and records 9 points on line 9 of the game sheet.

4. Play alternates to Team B. The roll is a 4 and a 4. This allows the team to delete either a 4 or an 8. Inasmuch as the 4 has been taken, the team deletes the 8. The team answers the question correctly and records 8 points on line 8 of the game sheet.

5. Play alternates to Team A, who rolls a 6 and a 5. The 5 has been deleted, but the 11 is available. Team A answers the question correctly and records 11 points on line 11 of the game sheet.

6. Play alternates to Team B. Team B rolls a 3 and a 4. The 4 has been deleted, as has the 7. Therefore, Team B cannot complete its roll, which completes play.

7. Team A, therefore, made the last complete dice roll and receives a bonus of 7 points. The final score then is Team A at 36 points and Team B at 8 points.

● CUSTOMIZING GAUNTLET

Regarding Group Size

- Accommodate larger groups by running several games simultaneously. Distribute a supply of questions to each game and have teams ask each other the questions.

Regarding Time

- Limit play to a designated amount of time or number of questions.

Regarding the Focus of the Task

- Allow each team to play independently. The team with the highest point total is declared the winner.

- Allow only the player who rolled the dice to answer the question.

- Allow a team to continue to roll the dice and answer questions until it answers a question incorrectly. Subtract the point value of the incorrect question from that team's total. Play then alternates to the other team. (*Note:* Teams should not deduct points below zero. Negative scores stigmatize learners.)

Regarding Scoring

- Give each team its own game sheet. Each team begins and continues to roll until its game sheet is depleted. The winner is the team with the most points.

GAME SHEET FOR
Gauntlet

· ·

Round #

Team A's Points	Correct Answer?	Dice Roll	Correct Answer?	Team B's Points
	If yes, record ◄—— score	1	If yes, record score ——►	
	If yes, record ◄—— score	2	If yes, record score ——►	
	If yes, record ◄—— score	3	If yes, record score ——►	
	If yes, record ◄—— score	4	If yes, record score ——►	
	If yes, record ◄—— score	5	If yes, record score ——►	
	If yes, record ◄—— score	6	If yes, record score ——►	
	If yes, record ◄—— score	7	If yes, record score ——►	
	If yes, record ◄—— score	8	If yes, record score ——►	
	If yes, record ◄—— score	9	If yes, record score ——►	
	If yes, record ◄—— score	10	If yes, record score ——►	
	If yes, record ◄—— score	11	If yes, record score ——►	
	If yes, record ◄—— score	12	If yes, record score ——►	
	7-point bonus? ◄——		7-point bonus? ——►	
	Score for Round #			

Jossey-Bass/Pfeiffer

Gauntlet

....

- **Team A rolls the dice.**

- **Team A crosses off numbers on the game sheet, either the sum of the dice or the two individual numbers.**

- **Team A answers a question. If correct, the team earns points corresponding to the numbers crossed off. If incorrect, the team records 0 points.**

- **Play alternates to Team B.**

- **Play continues until one team cannot complete its turn.**

Got a Minute?

• •

● PURPOSE

- To demonstrate how brainstorming techniques can approach real organizational problem solving.

- To develop the most uses for the item or topic mentioned in the randomly drawn category card.

- To re-energize a group with quick and playful brainstorming.

● SUPPLIES

- An overhead transparency or newsprint flip chart page of the Player Instructions for Got a Minute?, prepared in advance by the facilitator.

- An overhead projector (if using transparencies).

- A newsprint flip chart and felt-tipped markers.

- A deck of category cards, prepared in advance by the facilitator.

- A stopwatch or other timing device.

- Masking tape.

- Prizes (optional).

- A whistle or other noisemaking device.

● STEPS

1. Divide the group into teams of four to seven players each. Distribute several sheets of newsprint paper and a felt-tipped marker to each team.

2. Introduce the participants to four basic rules of brainstorming:

   - Do not critique others' ideas.

   - Do build on other ideas; there is no ownership of an idea.

   - Do go for the greatest number of ideas.

   - Do get outrageous; it is easier to tone down than create anew.

3. Define the task: "I will select one category card, at random, from this deck. Each team then has 60 seconds to identify as many ways as possible to respond to the statement I read. Record your ideas on the newsprint. When the time is up, each team will post its list and report on the items it recorded."

4. Post the Player Instructions, then select first card. Announce the topic and time the teams for 60 seconds. Call time at the end of 60 seconds.

5. Have each team in turn post and read its list aloud.

6. When all teams have reported, tally their scores, as follows:

   - Earn 5 points for each unique item.

   - Earn 1 point for each item found on another list.

7. Continue play in this manner for as many rounds as desired. The team with the most points when play ends is the winner.

SCORING EXAMPLE

1. The task was "Identify low/no-cost, positive ways to deal with customers at point-of-sale."

2. Team A's List: smile, give customer full attention, use customer's name, walk customer to item.

3. Team B's List: walk customer to item, establish eye contact, smile.

4. Score the lists as follows:

Team A

smile (on Team B's list)	1
give customer full attention	5
use customer's name	5
walk customer to item (on Team B's list)	1
Total	12 points

Team B

walk customer to item (on Team A's list)	1
establish eye contact	5
smile (on Team A's list)	1
Total	7 points

● CUSTOMIZING GOT A MINUTE?

Regarding Group Size

- Adjust the size of the teams and the number of teams to accommodate larger groups.

Regarding Time

- Play a designated number of rounds or until a specific time.

Regarding the Focus of the Task

- Allow other teams to challenge an item that is listed. If the challenge is successful, the challenged team loses 2 points. If the challenge is unsuccessful, the challenging team loses 5 points.

Regarding Scoring

- Award bonus points for especially unique items. The teams or the facilitator may act as judge.

Got a Minute?

....

- **The facilitator announces a category.**

- **Teams develop their lists.**

- **Teams post and report on their lists.**

- **Points are tallied as follows:**

  - **For each unique item, 5 points.**

  - **For each duplicate item, 1 point.**

  - **The team with the most points at the end wins.**

Headlines

. . . .

● PURPOSE

- To challenge the participants to create descriptions from brief statements of a topic or event.

- To demonstrate the group's understanding and/or perspective of a selected topic or event.

● SUPPLIES

- An overhead transparency or newsprint flip chart page of the Player Instructions for Headlines, prepared in advance by the facilitator.

- An overhead projector (if using transparencies).

- A newsprint flip chart and felt-tipped markers.

- A newsprint flip chart page with a sample headline, prepared in advance by the facilitator (e.g., "Deming Proposes 14-Point Program Based on Quality").

- Paper and pencils for the participants.

● STEPS

1. Divide the group into teams of one to five players each and distribute paper and pencils to each team.

2. Define the task: "You will be given a short headline that describes an event. Take ten minutes to develop a short article based on that headline. This is an open-book activity; you may use any resources to help you prepare your article."

3. Display the Player Instructions for Headlines and the sample headline.

4. After ten minutes, call time. Have each team in turn present its description.

5. Discuss and debrief the presentations as appropriate.

● CUSTOMIZING HEADLINES

Regarding Group Size

- Vary the number of teams according to the time allocated for this activity. The larger the number of teams, the longer the activity.

- Assign different teams to different headlines, particularly in large groups. This will broaden the scope of the material that can be reviewed and better maintain interest during the presentations.

Regarding Time

- Allow more or less time, depending on the complexity of the assignment.

- Place time limits on the presentations to match the available time.

Regarding the Focus of the Task

- Assign teams to create provocative headlines from readings or from handout material. (See "Bumper Stickers").

- Distribute a short article on the topic and have teams develop a series of short statements, a process used in story boarding.

Regarding Scoring

- Vote for a winner—the most original presentation, the most thorough, the most concise—and award prizes.

Headlines

....

- **Describe the event mentioned in the headline (10 minutes).**

- **Use any available resources.**

- **Present your description to the group.**

Hoops

●●●

● PURPOSE

- To allow participants to compete to answer questions and to score points.

● SUPPLIES

- An overhead transparency or newsprint flip chart page of the Player Instructions for Hoops, prepared in advance by the facilitator.

- A newsprint flip chart page of the Scoring Chart for Hoops, prepared in advance by the facilitator.

- An overhead projector (if using transparencies).

- A newsprint flip chart and felt-tipped markers.

- A set of questions, prepared in advance by the facilitator.

- Several sheets of paper, wadded into paper balls.

- Two baskets or cans (5" or 18 cm in diameter), large enough to hold the paper balls.

- Paper and pencils for the participants.

- Masking tape.

- A whistle or other noisemaking device.

● STEPS

1. Divide the group into two teams.

2. Set up two baskets or cans on a table as targets, with one at the near edge and the other at the farthest edge.

3. Set up shooting line with masking tape — a line from which players toss or "shoot" paper balls at the targets.

4. Define the task: "Each participant attempts to toss a paper ball into one of the targets. Then he or she responds to a question that I will ask. Points are awarded to the team based on the Scoring Chart."

5. Post and explain the Scoring Chart for Hoops.

6. Play alternates between teams: In each round, Team A sends a participant to toss a paper ball at the target and answer a question, then Team B follows suit.

7. After each question, post scores on a newsprint flip chart page.

8. After a designated number of rounds or a designated time limit, play ends. The team with the most points is declared the winner.

● SCORING EXAMPLE

1. A participant from Team A tosses a paper ball into the nearer target. He or she answers the facilitator's question correctly and scores 2 points for Team A.

2. A participant from Team B tosses a paper ball into the farther target. He or she answers the facilitator's question correctly and scores 3 points for Team B.

3. A participant from Team A aims a paper ball at a target, but misses. He or she answers the facilitator's question correctly and scores 1 point for Team A.

4. A participant from Team B answers the facilitator's question incorrectly. He or she scores 0 points for Team B, regardless of whether or not the paper ball went into the target.

● CUSTOMIZING HOOPS

Regarding Group Size

- Run two games simultaneously, with each team using some of the prepared questions to challenge its opponent.

Regarding Time

- Play to a predetermined number of points.

- Adjust the number of rounds of play.

Regarding the Focus of the Task

- Allow team members to confer about their answers.

- Permit "designated shooters"—players who are better at hitting the targets—to shoot for their teams each time, thereby raising the potential points scored.

Regarding Scoring

- Set up the targets at the same distance from the shooting line, but use targets of different sizes. The smaller target then is worth more points than the larger target.

- Designate a lightening round. Each team selects a player who shoots as many paper balls at the targets as possible in 30 seconds. Then the team is asked a question, and a correct response earns as many points as the number of balls that went into the target. An incorrect answer receives 0 points.

- Pose the same question to both teams. The first team to get a paper ball into a target answers the question. A correct answer scores 2 points, and an incorrect answer scores 0 points.

Hoops

....

- **Toss a paper ball at a target.**

- **Answer a question.**

- **Score points for the team based on the Scoring Chart.**

Hoops

- **Ball in farther target**
  AND correct answer = 3 points

- **Ball in nearer target**
  AND correct answer = 2 points

- **Ball misses target**
  AND correct answer = 1 point

- **Incorrect answer = 0 points**

Margin for Error

● ●

● **PURPOSE**

- To demonstrate an estimate-and-feedback process to involve participants in important numerical data.

- To demonstrate techniques and procedures for developing and analyzing numerical data.

● **SUPPLIES**

- An overhead transparency or newsprint flip chart page of the Player Instructions for Margin for Error, prepared in advance by the facilitator.

- An overhead projector (if using transparencies) or a newsprint flip chart and felt-tipped markers.

- A set of questions or clue statements, prepared in advance by the facilitator.

- Paper and pencils for the participants.

- A stopwatch or other timing device.

● **STEPS**

1. Divide the group into teams of five to seven players each, and post the Player Instructions.

2. Define the task: "You have been given a set of data relating to preparing a numerical estimate (such as a test market projection, projected sales figures,

etc. For example: develop an estimate of the density of the population in a projected test market. This would underscore target market population). Your team has three minutes in which to develop an estimate. You will be scored on which team comes closest to the actual figure."

3. After three minutes, call time and have each team in turn announce its estimate. Without revealing the actual answer, award points based on which team had the smallest margin of error (that is, which team was the closest, whether above or below the actual answer), as follows: The team with the smallest margin of error is awarded 10 points, the team with the next smallest margin of error is awarded 5 points, and the team with the third smallest margin of error is awarded 2 points.

4. Instruct the teams to spend one minute preparing another estimate. You may wish to give another clue or fact to help teams in their estimation process.

5. Call time and again award points based on the smallest margin of error.

6. Play as many rounds as are dictated by the importance of the data, the techniques of problem analysis being studied, or the proximity of the estimates.

7. At the end of the game, the team with the most points is declared the winner.

● CUSTOMIZING MARGIN FOR ERROR

Regarding Group Size

- Form as many groups as are needed to accommodate the participants.

Regarding Time

- Vary time requirements, allowing more time for more complicated problem statements or case studies.

- Call time after a specified number of rounds or a predetermined time period.

Regarding the Focus of the Task

- Use additional rounds of play to help groups "focus" in on the target number by sharing additional clues or facts. This can be done both during the scoring by offering suggestions of how to interpret data or in a "news flash" format that offers new information "just received by the company."

- Choose problem statements that reflect the kinds of data that the participants need to analyze, such as production runs, profit and cost projections, marketing and sales projections, and so on.

- Before hearing the estimates, select one team to present its estimate to the group. Allow the other teams to question and/or challenge. Ask each team to indicate whether or not it agrees that the presented estimate is the closest. Then award points as follows:

  If a team agrees AND this is the closest estimate, award 3 points.

  If a team disagrees AND this is the closest estimate, award 0 points.

  If a team agrees AND this is not the closest estimate, deduct 3 points.

  If a team disagrees AND this is not the closest estimate, award 3 points.

Regarding Scoring

- Use a point system that awards more points in later rounds, similar to the following:

Initial Round Estimates	Final Estimate
7 points for closest	11 points for closest
4 points for next closest	7 points for next closest
2 points for third closest	4 points for third closest

- Establish scoring based on pre-established margins of error, such as 10 points for estimates within 5 percent of the target; 5 points for estimates within 10 percent of the target; and 2 points for estimates within 15 percent of the target.

- Notify each team whether its estimate is over or under the target, as well as awarding points for the smallest margins of error.

Margin for Error

- **Each team makes its first estimate.**

- **Points are awarded based on the smallest margin of error.**

- **Each team makes a second estimate.**

- **Points are awarded based on the smallest margin of error.**

- **Play continues until the facilitator calls time.**

Message Board

● PURPOSE

- To allow participants to uncover clues about a prepared statement or message.

- To review topic material from lecture or readings.

● SUPPLIES

- An overhead transparency or newsprint flip chart page of the Player Instructions for Message Board, prepared in advance by the facilitator.

- An overhead projector (if using transparencies).

- A newsprint flip chart and felt-tipped markers.

- A set of questions, prepared in advance by the facilitator.

- One or more message boards prepared in advance on newsprint flip charts or wallboards, with message clues covered by Post-it™ notes or index cards.

- Paper and pencils for the participants.

● STEPS

1. Divide the group into two or three teams. Distribute paper and pencils to each team.

2. Define the task: "Your team's goal is to identify the message on the posted game board. The message board will be uncovered, one space at a time, as

teams provide correct answers to questions. When a team correctly answers the question, it receives one clue. A team may only guess at the message immediately after answering a question and receiving a clue."

3. Post the prepared message board and the Player Instructions.

4. Address the first question to Team A. If the team answers incorrectly, the question goes to the next team. If the team answers correctly, it can choose a clue to uncover on the message board. Once that clue is uncovered, the team has 30 seconds to guess at the message.

5. Play alternates to Team B. Again, if the team answers incorrectly, the question goes to the next team. If the team answers correctly, it can choose a clue to uncover on the message board. Once that clue is uncovered, the team has 30 seconds to guess at the message.

6. Play continues until one team correctly identifies the message. That team is declared the winner of that round of play.

● CUSTOMIZING MESSAGE BOARD

Regarding Group Size

- For larger groups, prepare several message boards, then divide the group into teams of four or five members each. Assign each team to create a set of topic-focused questions and attach these to the outer surface of the message board. When the teams have completed their message boards, put three teams together and have each team in turn present its prepared questions and the message board to the other two teams.

Regarding Time

- Increase or decrease the number of clues on the message board.

- Set time limits for teams to answer their questions and make their guesses.

Regarding the Focus of the Task

- Prepare sets of questions in different categories of your topic. Attach the category to the outer surface of the message board. Allow teams to select a category and then provide the question indicated by the category. If correct, uncover that portion of the board, then allow the team 30 seconds to guess the message. If the guess is incorrect, play passes to the next team. Continue play until one team correctly identifies the message from the board.

Use the inner board in three ways: (1) to show clues that will identify the final message—muscle relaxation, meditation, breathe deeply, vitamins C and B, eight glasses of water daily, proper diet, reduce fat intake, proper exercise, reduce caffeine intake = "ways to reduce stress," (2) to show message bits that, when pieced together, call for an answer—name + three + ways to + reduce + bioecological + stress level + by changes + in nutrition + and diet. Answer: reduce alcohol, increase water intake, reduce caffeine, reduce fat, increase fiber, reduce drugs, etc., and (3) to show letters that form a word—(clue: caffeine, for one)—s.t.i.m.u.l.a.n.t.

Regarding Scoring

- Award 1 point for each question that is answered correctly; subtract 1 point for each incorrect guess. Award a 5-point bonus for solving the puzzle.

Message Board

- The first team answers a question.

- If the answer is incorrect, play passes to the next team.

- A correct answer uncovers a clue.

- The team has 30 seconds to guess the message.

- Play alternates to the next team.

- The team that guesses the message wins the round.

Sample Message Board

Muscle relaxation	Meditation	Breathe deeply
Vitamins C and B	Eight glasses of water daily	Proper diet
Reduce fat intake	Proper exercise	Reduce caffeine intake

Message: "Ways to Cope with Stress"

Nothing Ventured

● PURPOSE

- To allow teams to answer questions and earn points based on the roll of dice.

- To review topic material from lecture or readings

● SUPPLIES

- An overhead transparency or newsprint flip chart page of the Player Instructions for Nothing Ventured, prepared in advance by the facilitator.

- An overhead projector (if using transparencies) or a newsprint flip chart and felt-tipped markers.

- A set of questions, prepared in advance by the facilitator.

- One copy of the Game Sheet for Nothing Ventured for each team.

- One die per team.

- Paper and pencils for the participants.

● STEPS

1. Divide the group into teams of three to five players each. Distribute a game sheet and a die to each team.

2. Define the task: "This game is played in a series of dice rolls. Each team rolls its die, then it is given a question. If it provides a correct answer, the die roll is

added to the team's point total. If the answer is incorrect, the die roll is subtracted from the team's point total. The team with the most points at the end of play is the winner."

3. Post the Player Instructions and begin the game.

4. The team with the most points at the end of play is declared the winner.

● SCORING EXAMPLE

1. Team A rolls a 5 and answers its question correctly. Team A records 5 points on first line of its game sheet. Team A's total is 5 points. (*Note:* If Team A's answer were incorrect, its score would be –5 points.)

2. Team A rolls a 4 and provides an incorrect answer. Team A records –4 points on the second line of the game sheet. Team A's total is 5 – 4 points = 1 point.

3. Team A rolls a 3 and provides a correct answer. Team A adds 3 points on the third line of the game sheet. Team A's total is 1 + 3 points = 4 points.

4. Team A rolls a 1 and provides an incorrect answer. Team A records –1 point on the fourth line of the game sheet. Team A's total is 4 – 1 point = 3 points.

● CUSTOMIZING NOTHING VENTURED

Regarding Group Size

- Accommodate any number of players by increasing or decreasing the number of teams or the size of the teams.

Regarding Time

- Limit the time allowed for answering questions.

- Play for a specified length of time or number of rounds.

Regarding the Focus of the Task

- Arrange the difficulty or complexity of the questions by the number of the die, with one being the simplest and six the most challenging.

Regarding Scoring

- Allow teams to choose to double their die roll before hearing the question.

- Use questions of varying difficulty and award double or triple points for more difficult questions.

GAME SHEET FOR
Nothing Ventured

• •

Team Name

Question	Die Roll	Answer	Correct or Incorrect?	Points Scored	Total
1.					
2.					
3.					
4.					
5.					
6.					
7.					
8.					
9.					
10.					
11.					
12.					

Jossey-Bass/Pfeiffer

PLAYER INSTRUCTIONS FOR
Nothing Ventured

- **Roll die and record the roll.**

- **Answer the question.**

- **Record scores.**

- **If correct, add the number to the score.**

- **If incorrect, deduct the number from the score.**

One Potato

∙∙∙

● PURPOSE

- To offer players an opportunity to answer questions and earn varying numbers of points.

- To review topic material from lecture or readings.

● SUPPLIES

- An overhead transparency or newsprint flip chart page of the Player Instructions for One Potato, prepared in advance by the facilitator.

- An overhead projector (if using transparencies) or a newsprint flip chart and felt-tipped markers.

- A set of questions, prepared in advance by the facilitator.

- Paper and pencils for participants.

- One copy of the Game Sheet for One Potato for each participant.

● STEPS

1. Have each participant choose a partner. Designate one player as "odds" and the other player as "evens," and give each player a game sheet.

2. Define the task: "This game is played in rounds. Before each round you and your partner will put out one or two fingers. The number of points you receive for a correct answer will be determined by who wins the odds-or-

evens finger throw. If the total number of fingers shown is three, the "odds" player scores 2 points for a correct answer and the "evens" player scores 1 point for a correct answer. If the total number of fingers shown is two or four, the "odds" player receives 1 point for a correct answer and the "evens" player receives 2 points for a correct answer. Incorrect answers always receive 0 points. The winner is the player with the most points at the end of the game."

3. Post the Player Instructions and instruct partners to show one or two fingers.

4. Both players record the outcome—"odds" or "evens"—on their game sheets. When the question is asked, both players answer on their own game sheets.

5. Give the correct answer, and have the players record the number of points they earned on their game sheets.

6. For each subsequent round, have players put out their fingers, record the tally, answer the question, and score points for each correct answer. At the end of play, the player with the most points is declared the winner.

● SCORING EXAMPLE

1. In round one, three fingers were shown. This means that the "odds" player receives 2 points for a correct answer, and the "evens" player receives 1 point for a correct answer. The "odds" player gave the correct answer and earned 2 points; the "evens" player also gave the correct answer and earned 1 point.

2. In round two, two fingers were shown. This means that the "odds" player receives 1 point for a correct answer, and the "evens" player receives 2 points for a correct answer. However, both players gave incorrect answers, and both earned 0 points.

● CUSTOMIZING ONE POTATO

Regarding Group Size

- Allow any number of pairs of players to play simultaneously. With an odd number of participants, form one group of three and designate the third person as "odds" also.

Jossey-Bass/Pfeiffer

Regarding Time

- Play a specified number of rounds or for a specific length of time.

- Limit the amount of time that players have to answer questions.

Regarding the Focus of the Task

- Use open-ended questions. Have one pair of players read their responses aloud and allow the other participants to vote on the better answer. That person receives the appropriate number of points, and the other player receives no points.

- Use the game with individual players.

Regarding Scoring

- Allow players to opt for doubling the value of the question before showing their fingers and hearing the question.

GAME SHEET FOR
One Potato

....

Instructions:

- If the tally of fingers is three, the "odds" player receives 2 points for a correct answer, and the "evens" player receives 1 point for a correct answer.

- If the tally of fingers is two or four, the "odds" player receives 1 point for a correct answer, and the "evens" player receives 2 points for a correct answer.

	Answer	Tally	Points
1.			
2.			
3.			
4.			
5.			
6.			
7.			
8.			
9.			
10.			

PLAYER INSTRUCTIONS FOR
One Potato

· ·

- **Find a partner.**

- **Designate one player as "odds" and one player as "evens."**

- **Show one or two fingers each, and record the total.**

- **Answer the question asked.**

- **Record points on the game sheet.**

- **Incorrect answers receive 0 points.**

Penny Wise

● ●

● PURPOSE

- To offer teams an opportunity to throw pennies to determine pay-off and then answer questions for points.

- To review topic material from lecture or readings

● SUPPLIES

- An overhead transparency or newsprint flip chart page of the Player Instructions for Penny Wise, prepared in advance by the facilitator.

- An overhead projector (if using transparencies).

- A newsprint flip chart and felt-tipped markers.

- A set of questions, prepared in advance by the facilitator.

- Paper and pencils for the participants.

- One copy of the Game Sheet for Penny Wise for each team.

- One copy of the Score Sheet for Penny Wise to explain scoring for each penny toss.

- Three pennies for each pair of teams.

- One paper cup for each pair of teams.

- A whistle or other noisemaking device.

● STEPS

1. Divide the group into teams of two to three players each.

2. Pair up teams, and have each team select either heads or tails.

3. Distribute the game materials—two copies of the score sheet, one paper cup, and three pennies.

4. Define the task: "This game is played in rounds. Before each round, place three pennies in your cup, then toss them on the table. Record the status of the throw on the game sheet. You will be asked a question. A correct answer earns the number of points shown on the game sheet."

5. Post the Player Instructions, and begin the game.

6. Play continues for a specified number of rounds, or until time is called.

7. The team with the most points when play ends is the winner.

● SCORING EXAMPLE

1. The teams at Table 1 toss the pennies and have two heads and one tail. Both teams check the "HHT" designation on the game sheet.

2. The facilitator reads a question. Both teams record their answers on line 1 of their game sheets.

3. The facilitator reads the answer. The "heads" team answers correctly and receives 2 points. The "tails" team answers incorrectly and receives 0 points.

4. The teams at Table 2 toss their pennies and have three tails. Both teams check the "TTT" designation on their game sheets.

5. The facilitator reads question 2. Both teams record their answers on line 2 of the game sheet.

6. The facilitator reads the answer. The "tails" team answers correctly and receives 3 points. This completes this round of play.

7. The teams at Table 3 toss their pennies and have three heads. Both teams check the "HHH" designator on their game sheets.

8. The facilitator reads question 3. Both teams record their answers on line 3 of the game sheet.

9. The facilitator reads the answer. The "heads" team answers incorrectly and receives 0 points. The "tails" team answers correctly and receives 3 points.

● CUSTOMIZING PENNY WISE

Regarding Group Size

- Adjust the size of the teams and the number of teams to accommodate the size of the group.

- Conduct several games simultaneously by having pairs of teams compete with each other, all answering the same questions.

Regarding Time

- Limit the amount of time that teams have to answer the questions.

- Play for a specified period of time.

Regarding the Focus of the Task

- Use the game with individual players.

Regarding Scoring

- Allow teams the option of doubling the point value of the round before tossing the pennies.

- Establish penalties for incorrect answers so that teams can lose points.

SCORE SHEET FOR FACILITATOR
Penny Wise

• •

Penny Toss Shows	Correct Team Answer	Incorrect Team Answer
heads-heads-tails	heads team: 2 points tails team: 1 point	0 points
tails-tails-heads	heads team: 1 point tails team: 2 points	0 points
heads-heads-heads	heads team: 3 points*** tails team: 0 points	0 points
tails-tails-tails	heads team: 0 points*** tails team: 3 points	0 points

*** Note that if the answering team provides an incorrect answer to a 3-point question, opponents may take the points by providing the correct answer.

Penny Wise

. . . .

Coins Show:	"H" Team	"T" Team	Incorrect Answers
HHT correct answer earns	2 points	1 point	0 points
TTH correct answer earns	1 point	2 points	0 points
HHH correct answer earns	3 points	0 points*	0 points
TTT correct answer earns	0 points*	3 points	0 points

* If answering team misses 3-point question, opponents make take the points by correctly answering the question.

Answer		H	T
1.	HHT TTH HHH TTT		
2.	HHT TTH HHH TTT		
3.	HHT TTH HHH TTT		
4.	HHT TTH HHH TTT		
5.	HHT TTH HHH TTT		
6.	HHT TTH HHH TTT		
7.	HHT TTH HHH TTT		
8.	HHT TTH HHH TTT		
9.	HHT TTH HHH TTT		
10.	HHT TTH HHH TTT		
	Total Score		

Penny Wise

- Select "heads" and "tails" teams.

- Toss pennies and record on the game sheet.

- The facilitator asks a question.

- Both teams record their answers on the game sheet.

- Points are awarded according to the chart on the game sheet.

Pop Quiz

● PURPOSE

  • To review material from lectures or readings with speed and accuracy.

● SUPPLIES

  • An overhead transparency or newsprint flip chart page of the Player Instructions for Pop Quiz, prepared in advance by the facilitator.

  • An overhead projector (if using transparencies) or a newsprint flip chart and felt-tipped markers.

  • A set of question cards for each subgroup, prepared in advance by the facilitator.

  • One copy of the Game Sheet for Pop Quiz for each team.

  • Paper and pencils for the participants.

  • Several three-ounce paper cups for each team. (*Note:* Some facilitators use one tennis ball per team because they feel it is easier for players to cover and hold on to during game play.)

● STEPS

  1. Divide the group into subgroups of three to five players each. Seat each subgroup at its own table, and distribute materials: a set of question cards, a copy of the game sheet, paper, pencils, and several paper cups.

2. Define the task: "List each player's name in the columns across the top of your game sheet. Place a paper cup in the middle of the table, where all of the members of your subgroup can reach it. When play begins, Player 1 will read the first question card. The other members of the subgroup decide on their answers and compete to be the first to cover the paper cup with their hand. The first player to cover the paper cup is eligible to answer the question. If that player is correct, he or she receives 1 point; if the player is incorrect, he or she loses 1 point. Points are recorded in the appropriate column on the game sheet. Play then rotates clockwise to another subgroup member, who reads the next question."

3. Post the Player Instructions and instruct the subgroups to begin their games.

4. At the end of play, the player in each subgroup with the most points wins. The player among the whole group who has the most points is declared the grand prize winner.

● CUSTOMIZING POP QUIZ

Regarding Group Size

- Run as many subgroup competitions as needed to accommodate the group.

- Centralize the question process with small groups by asking the questions yourself and having subgroups track their own scores.

Regarding Time

- Limit the number of rounds or specify a time frame for the activity.

- Place time limits on how long a player has to answer a question.

Regarding the Focus of the Task

- Allow challenges. After the first player gives an answer, but before hearing the correct answer, other players may challenge with other answers. Award points for the correct answers and penalize the incorrect answers. For example:

  If the first player's answer is correct, the challenging players each lose 3 points.

If the first player's answer is incorrect and the challenging player's answer is correct, the challenger earns 5 points.

If the first player's answer is incorrect and the challenging player's answer is incorrect, the challenger earns 1 point.

- Instruct the players who do not reach the cup first to write down their answers to the question. If the first player's answer is wrong, award points to others for correct answers.

- Place a paper cup on one table in a central location. Give each subgroup identical problem statements. The first team who sends a player to touch the cup is eligible to answer the problem statement. The facilitator responds with the correct solution and rewards or penalizes the answering team.

- For special tournament play, substitute a raw egg for the paper cup. Be sure that players are in casual clothing and that the playing table is covered with a disposable cloth or paper. Note any variations in game play in terms of intensity and quality of play. Then debrief players on the consequences of introducing a mess-producing item into play.

Regarding Scoring

- Vary the rewards for correct answers and the penalties for incorrect answers, based on the difficulty of the question or to add more impact to the game. For example, every fifth question could be worth double or triple credit.

GAME SHEET FOR
Pop Quiz

Player's Name
_____

Question #
_____

Total
_____

Question #	Player's Name					
Total Score						

Jossey-Bass/Pfeiffer

Pop Quiz

··

- **Players take turns reading questions.**

- **The first player to cover the paper cup is eligible to answer the question.**

- **If the answer is correct, the player receives 1 point.**

- **If the answer is incorrect, the player loses 1 point.**

- **The player with the most points at the end of the game wins.**

Question of Identity

● PURPOSE

- To allow participants to use team questioning and deductive reasoning to discover a topic.

- To demonstrate group problem solving while reinforcing material from lecture and readings.

● SUPPLIES

- An overhead transparency or newsprint flip chart page of the Player Instructions for Question of Identity, prepared in advance by the facilitator.

- An overhead projector (if using transparencies).

- A newsprint flip chart and felt-tipped markers.

- A list of objects to be identified, prepared in advance by the facilitator.

- Paper and pencils for the participants.

● STEPS

1. Divide the group into two or three teams.

2. Define the task: "Find the mystery item by asking questions that can answered by "yes" or "no." Each team may ask one question per turn, and each question costs 1 point. Each team may attempt one solution per turn, and each attempt

costs 1 point. The team that guesses the item correctly has 5 points deducted from its score. The object of the game is to finish with as few points as possible."

3. Post the Player Instructions and identify a category for the item to be identified (e.g., person, process, event, etc.).

4. The first team asks one question that can be answered with "yes" or "no." The team then has the option to try to guess the item or to end its turn. Each question costs the team 1 point, and each attempt to guess the item also costs the team 1 point. Note each question and its answer on a newsprint flip chart page, also tracking the points that each team accumulates.

5. Each team in turn asks questions and attempts to guess the item. Play ends when a team guesses the item correctly. At this point, the team with the fewest points wins.

● SAMPLE PLAY

After dividing the class into three teams, the facilitator writes the following heads on a flip-chart page: "Team 1," "Team 2," and "Team 3." The facilitator then posts the following clue: "This is a final product made by the batch production process."

Round 1. The first team asks, "Is it a food product?" The facilitator writes "food?" on the flip chart and answers "no." The first team is invited to guess at the product. The team declines. The first team is then charged 1 point, which is posted by the facilitator under "Team 1."

The second team asks, "Is it a pharmaceutical product?" The facilitator writes "pharmaceutical?" on the flip chart and then answers "no." The second team is invited to guess at the product. The team declines. The second team is charged 1 point, which is posted by the facilitator under "Team 2."

The third team asks, "Is it an automobile?" The facilitator writes "automobile?" on the flip chart and then answers "no," adding that an automobile is made by the fabrication process, not batch. The third team is invited to guess at the product. The team declines. The third team is charged 1 point, which is posted by the facilitator under "Team 3."

This ends the first round.

Round 2. The first team asks, "Is it an oil-based product?" The facilitator writes "oil?" on the flip chart and answers "yes." The first team is invited to guess the product. The team accepts and guesses: "Is it gasoline?" The facilitator writes "gasoline?" on the flip chart and then answers "no." The first team is charged 1 point for the question and 1 point for the guess for a round total of 2 points. The first team now has a game total of 3 points, which is posted by the facilitator under "Team 1."

The second team asks, "Is it used around the house?" The facilitator writes "used around house?" on the flip chart and answers "no," adding that it can sometimes be found around the house, but it is not usually used by the home owner. The second team is invited to guess at the product. The team accepts and guesses: "Is it diesel fuel?" The facilitator writes "diesel fuel?" and then answers "no." The second team is charged 1 point for the question and 1 point for the guess for a round total of 2 points. The second team now has a game total of 3 points, which is posted by the facilitator under "Team 2."

The third team asks, "Is the product used to drive or run any machinery?" The facilitator writes "run machinery?" on the flip chart and then answers "no." The third team is invited to guess at the product. The team accepts and guesses: "Is it asphalt?" The facilitator writes "asphalt?" on the flip chart and then answers "yes!" The third team is charged 1 point for the question and 1 point for the guess, and then 5 points are deducted for the correct solution for a round total of –3 points. The third team has a game total of –2 points, which is posted by the facilitator under "Team 3." Team 3 is declared the winner.

● CUSTOMIZING QUESTION OF IDENTITY

Regarding Group Size

- For larger groups, enlist participants to serve as leaders and run several games simultaneously. Each leader uses an item from the list previously prepared by the facilitator and works with two teams.

Regarding Time

- Put time limits on how long teams have to ask their questions and attempt their guesses.

- Designate the number of rounds of play or specify the time frame for the activity.

Regarding the Focus of the Game

- Have teams predict how many questions it will take to identify the item and award points accordingly.

- Post clues after each round to help teams focus on an answer.

- Use this activity to enhance and reinforce the subject matter of your particular training session.

- Debrief the activity afterward, focusing on teamwork and problem solving.

Regarding Scoring

- Charge 1 point for each question that receives a "yes" answer and 2 points for each question that receives a "no" answer.

Question of Identity

....

- Team A asks a question.

- The facilitator answers "yes" or "no."

- Team A attempts to guess the item (optional).

- Team A is charged 1 point for its question and another 1 point if it attempted a guess.

- Play alternates to the next team.

- Play continues until one team guesses the item.

- The team that guesses the item has 5 points deducted from its score.

- The team with the lowest score wins.

Shape Up!

• •

● PURPOSE

- To establish a problem-solving climate and to bring participants into problem-solving groups.

● SUPPLIES

- An overhead transparency or newsprint flip chart page of the Player Instructions for Shape Up!, prepared in advance by the facilitator.

- An overhead projector (if using transparencies) or a newsprint flip chart and felt-tipped markers.

- A set of task assignments (see the sample at the end of this game), prepared in advance by the facilitator as follows:

Determine the number of task assignments you want resolved and choose a shape for each task.

Write the tasks you wish each subgroup to accomplish on the appropriate shape.

Determine the number of participants you want in each subgroup. Then cut the shapes into the appropriate number of irregular pieces. For example, if you want four members in each subgroup, you would cut each shape into four pieces. If you want five members in each subgroup, you would cut the shape into five pieces.

Let's say you have four tasks; this would then require four different shapes. If you want four members in each subgroup, you would cut each shape into four pieces. For a group of thirty-two, you should prepare two colors of each shape—circles, hearts, rectangles, and squares—cut into four irregular pieces. Thus, you would have two subgroups working on each task.

- Paper and pencils for the participants.

● STEPS

1. Define the task: "Each of you will receive a piece of a shape. You must find the participants who have other pieces that are the same color as yours and that complete the shape. When you find the other participants and assemble your shape, begin the task that is written on the shape. You will have two minutes to complete the task."

2. Post the Player Instructions and hand out the previously prepared shapes, along with paper and pencils.

3. Call time at the end of two minutes. Have each subgroup in turn report on its task assignment and its solution. Award 1 point for each item developed.

4. The subgroup with the most points is declared the winner.

5. Debrief and discuss the activity as warranted.

● CUSTOMIZING SHAPE UP!

Regarding Group Size

- Regulate the number of subgroups by the number of shapes and pieces used. (See instructions in the Supplies section at the beginning of this game.)

Regarding Time

- Allow more or less time for the activity, depending on the complexity of the task assignments.

Regarding the Focus of the Task

- Choose task assignments that complement the rest of the planned training session.

- Omit one piece from each shape to determine how participants handle ambiguity.

- Focus the debrief questions around identifying which participants took leadership and the results.

- Switch task assignments after each subgroup has reported. Assign another subgroup to expand on the solutions devised by the original problem-solving group.

Regarding Scoring

- Allow the group to vote for the most creative or most practical solutions and award prizes.

Shape Up!

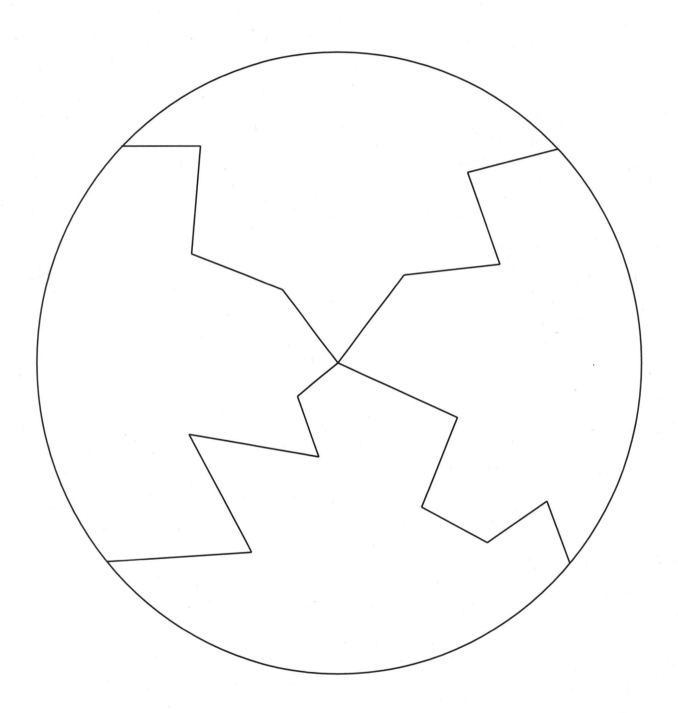

Shape Up!

....

- **Find the other players whose shapes complete yours.**

- **Work on the task written on the shape.**

- **Present your conclusions to the entire group.**

- **Your subgroup receives 1 point for each idea it generates.**

Shape Up!

SAMPLE RESPONSES:

willingness to help

sincere or caring

timely service

resolve complaints

listening skills

smiles

polite

knowledge of product

patient

attentive

accountability

personalized service

use customer's name

ask questions

Six Pack

. . . .

● PURPOSE

- To allow participants to answer review questions in categories determined by rolls on a die.

● SUPPLIES

- An overhead transparency or newsprint flip chart page of the Player Instructions for Six Pack, prepared in advance by the facilitator.

- An overhead projector (if using transparencies).

- A newsprint flip chart and felt-tipped markers.

- A newsprint flip chart page listing the six categories of questions that will be used in the game, prepared in advance by the facilitator.

- Six sets of questions, one for each of the selected categories, prepared in advance by the facilitator.

- One copy of the Game Sheet for Six Pack for each team.

- One die.

- Paper and pencils for the participants.

- A whistle or other noisemaker.

● STEPS

1. Divide the group into teams of three to five players each.

2. Distribute one copy of the game sheet, paper, and pencils to each team.

3. Post the Player Instructions and the newsprint sheet that lists the categories for this game.

4. Define the task: "I have prepared questions in the following six categories: [name and point out on the posted newsprint]. I will roll a die to determine the category of the question, and then I will ask the question. Your team will have one minute to decide on its answer to the question and to write the answer on your game sheet. If your answer is correct, your team scores 1 point. If your answer is incorrect, your team loses 1 point. The team with the most points at the end of the game wins."

5. Begin play by rolling a die and asking a question from the category that corresponds to that roll of the die. Allow teams one minute to decide on their answers; then announce the correct answer. Teams track their own scores on their game sheets. Play continues for a predetermined number of rounds or specified time limit.

6. At the end of play, the team with the most points wins.

● CUSTOMIZING SIX PACK

Regarding Group Size

- Accommodate larger groups by increasing the size of the teams or by increasing the number of teams.

- Accommodate smaller groups by decreasing the size of the teams or by decreasing the number of teams.

Regarding Time

- Set in advance a specific time limit for length of play. The team with the highest score at that point wins.

- Vary the time allowed for teams to answer based on the difficulty of the material.

Regarding the Focus of the Task

- Once the category has been determined, allow teams to bid on how many points they are willing to risk on the upcoming question.

- Select a topic area by a roll of the die. Require each team to list multiple answers or options to the question within a specified time limit. Each correct answer earns 1 point, and each incorrect answer scores 0 points.

Regarding Scoring

- Prepare questions at various levels of difficulty, and assign point values to each one. For example, you might announce "The next question is in the customer service category, and it is worth 3 points."

GAME SHEET FOR
Six Pack

Team Name

	Die Roll	Category	Correct Answer?	Points	Total
1					
2					
3					
4					
5					
6					
7					
8					
9					
10					
11					
12					

Jossey-Bass/Pfeiffer

Six Pack

- Each roll of the die determines the category of a question.

- Your team has one minute to write its answer to the question.

- Correct answers earn 1 point.

- Incorrect answers lose 1 point.

- The team with the most points at the end of the game wins.

Stretch Mark

. . . .

● PURPOSE

- To motivate teams to stretch their creativity to come up with multiple solutions to a problem statement.

- To promote a problem-solving environment.

● SUPPLIES

- An overhead transparency or newsprint flip chart page of the Player Instructions for Stretch Mark, prepared in advance by the facilitator.

- An overhead projector (if using transparencies).

- A newsprint flip chart and felt-tipped markers.

- A set of problem statements, prepared in advance by the facilitator.

- Paper and pencils for the participants.

● STEPS

1. Divide the group into teams of three to five players each. Distribute paper and pencils to each team.

2. Define the task: "I will read a problem statement. Your team will have three minutes to propose solutions to the problem. The first solution you propose will earn your team 1 point; the second solution will earn 2 points; the third

solution will earn 3 points; and so on. The only limit to the points that can be earned is your creativity and your willingness to stretch your problem-solving skills."

3. Post the Player Instructions, read the problem statement, and instruct the teams to begin.

4. After three minutes, call time. Have each team in turn read its list of proposed solutions. Award points as indicated in the Scoring Example that follows.

5. Continue for as many rounds as desired. The team with the most points at the end of play is declared the winner.

● SCORING EXAMPLE

1. The problem statement is "There has been a slight decrease in first-quarter sales. Develop ways to increase customer satisfaction with minimal cost."

2. Team A develops 17 proposed solutions. Team A's point total is as follows: $1 + 2 + 3 + 4 + 5 + 6 + 7 + 8 + 9 + 10 + 11 + 12 + 13 + 14 + 15 + 16 + 17 = 153$ points.

● CUSTOMIZING STRETCH MARK

Regarding Group Size

- Vary the number and size of the teams to suit the size of the group.

- Prepare two problem statements and have half of the teams work on the first problem and the other half of the teams work on the second problem.

Regarding Time

- Modify the time allotted to develop solutions based on the complexity of the problem.

- Adjust the time frames to fit the time available.

Regarding the Focus of the Task

- Allow teams to challenge one another's solutions. Based on how convincing the arguments are, the facilitator awards or deducts points.

- Ask each team to rank its solutions, listing the "best three," "strangest three," "most affordable three," or any other applicable criterion.

Regarding Scoring

- Batch the scoring, assigning 1 point for each of the first five solutions, 2 points for each of the next five solutions, and so on.

- Prepare a list of the solutions proposed by more than one team. Work with the participants to rank order these options from most likely to least likely. Then add bonus points to the teams that proposed the top three solutions.

Stretch Mark

- Develop solutions to address the problem statement.

- Earn 1 point for the first solution you list.

- Earn 2 points for the second solution you list.

- Earn 3 points for the third solution you list and so on.

- The team with the most points wins.

Test Match

● PURPOSE

- To experience different testing formats in a nonthreatening environment.

- To predict how many questions each team can answer pertaining to a certain topic.

● SUPPLIES

- An overhead transparency or newsprint flip chart page of the Player Instructions for Test Match, prepared in advance by the facilitator.

- A newsprint flip chart page for the scoring for Test Match, prepared in advance by the facilitator.

- An overhead projector (if using transparencies).

- A newsprint flip chart and felt-tipped markers.

- One Test Sheet for each player, prepared in advance by the facilitator.

- Paper and pencil for each participant.

● STEPS

1. Divide the group into teams of two players each.

2. Distribute paper and pencils to each team.

3. Define the task: "Each team is to estimate how many correct answers it will provide to the test questions. The object is to be the team that both (1) has the highest original estimate and (2) matches or exceeds that estimate. I will list the scores on the flip chart. You will have five minutes to answer the questions on the test."

4. Display the Player Instructions for Test Match and the estimated scores.

5. Distribute one test sheet to each player on the team. You may want to remind players that only one answer per question will be accepted from each team.

6. Go over the test. Have each team tally its number of correct answers.

7. Post each team's final score next to the original estimate.

8. The team with the highest final score that exceeds or matches its original estimate score is declared the winner.

● SCORING EXAMPLE FOR FIVE QUESTION TEST MATCH

1. Team A estimates that it will provide 4 correct answers. During the test it provides four correct answers.

2. Team B estimates that it will provide 5 correct answers. During the test it provides 4 correct answers.

3. Team C estimates that it will provide 4 correct answers. During the test it provides 5 correct answers.

4. Team D estimates that it will provide 5 correct answers. During the test it provides 5 correct answers.

5. Team D is declared the winner because it had the highest original estimate (5 correct answers), which it matched or exceeded. Teams A and C only estimated 4 correct answers. Only Team D took the highest original risk and met or exceeded that estimate.

● CUSTOMIZING TEST MATCH

Regarding Group Size

- This game can be used for almost any size group, but it is more effective for groups larger than twelve.

Regarding Time

- Extend the time in proportion to the number of questions on the test. For short-answer questions, allow one to two minutes per question. Allow more time for more complex, analytical, or technical questions.

Regarding the Focus of the Task

- Consider using this game as an introduction to new material. By pairing players in teams and emphasizing the game format, players will become intrigued with the learning and not feel threatened.

- Introduce new material that may appear in later examinations to allow players to both preview the information and learn techniques on how to take post-criterion or standardized tests.

- Allow players to use books or other desk references in an "open book" environment. This can underscore the value of take-home readings.

- After players complete the test, have teams "revise" original estimates. This allows players to reflect on how well they did on the test. But, the facilitator should remind teams that only the original estimate counts in determining the winner.

Regarding Scoring

- Apply extra weight to questions of extra complexity or importance.

- Use "brackets" when recording the original estimates to simplify the task. Thus, estimates for a seven-question test would be recorded as follows: 6–7 correct, 4–5 correct, and 1–3 correct.

Test Match

- **Estimate the number of questions you will answer correctly.**

- **Answer the questions.**

- **Each team tallies its final score.**

- **Team with the highest original estimate and whose score matches or exceedes its original estimate is declared the winner.**

Jossey-Bass/Pfeiffer

SAMPLE TEST SHEET FOR
Test Match

· ·

Test Match: Stress Management

Instructions:

• Estimate how many questions you will answer correctly.

• Register your estimate in the space below.

• When instructed, begin test.

• Only one answer per team is valid.

Estimate [   ]

1. Drinking warm water is preferable to drinking cold water. True or False?

2. What beverage is the most frequently consumed source of caffeine in the American diet?

3. What is the best way to calm down in a stressful situation—express your feelings, drink alcohol, or breathe deeply?

4. Name the type of aerobic exercise that relies on keeping one foot on the floor at all times—step aerobics, low-impact aerobics, or fitness walking.

5. Who enjoys better health—married or single people?

Answer Key (for the facilitator)

1. False. Cold water is absorbed into your system more quickly than warm water. Also, there is evidence to suggest that drinking cold water can actually help burn calories.

2. Coffee. Americans over the age of 14 consume an average of 3 cups per day.

3. Breathe deeply. Diaphragmatic or "stomach" breathing helps you control your body functions and relax.

4. Low-impact aerobics. Low-impact routines rely on keeping one foot on the floor at all times, thereby reducing the jarring effects of hops, jumps, and skips.

5. Married people. A recent survey showed that mortality was lower among married people as compared with single, widowed, and divorced individuals of all races.

Tic-Tac-Two

● ●

● PURPOSE

- To allow teams to answer questions and select spaces to get three spaces in a row.

- To review topic material from lecture or readings.

● SUPPLIES

- An overhead transparency or newsprint flip chart page of the Player Instructions for Tic-Tac-Two, prepared in advance by the facilitator.

- An overhead projector (if using transparencies) or a newsprint flip chart and felt-tipped markers.

- A set of questions, prepared in advance by the facilitator.

- One Game Sheet for Tic-Tac-Two for each pair of teams.

- Twelve poker chips for each pair of teams, six red and six white.

- Paper and pencils for the participants.

● STEPS

1. Divide the group into teams of two to three players each. Pair up the teams (a red team and a white team), and distribute one game board and twelve poker chips to each pair of teams.

---

2. Define the task: "The red team will be asked a question. If the team responds correctly, it may select and cover a space on the game sheet with a red chip. If the team selects the center space, it must correctly answer a second question. If the team answers incorrectly, play alternates to the white team. Play continues until one team gets three chips in a row, horizontally, vertically, or diagonally."

3. Post the Player Instructions and begin with a question for the red teams.

4. Play continues until one team has three chips in a row.

● CUSTOMIZING TIC-TAC-TWO

Regarding Group Size

- Accommodate groups of any size by varying the number of teams and the size of the teams.

Regarding Time

- Set time limits for teams to answer questions.

- Play for a specific length of time or number of rounds.

Regarding the Focus of the Task

- Have both teams write down their answers to all questions. If the team whose turn it is answers incorrectly, the other team may submit its answer. If the second team is correct, it may cover its opponent's space for this round and still have its turn in the next round.

Regarding Scoring

- Vary the difficulty of the questions and allow two spaces to be selected with the more difficult questions.

- Have teams select and use the letteres "X" and "O" to cover spaces. This eliminates the need for poker chips.

Tic-Tac-Two

PLAYER INSTRUCTIONS FOR
Tic-Tac-Two

- Pair up teams.

- The first team answers a question.

- If correct, the team covers a space.

- If incorrect, play alternates to the other team.

- Continue play until one team covers three spaces in a row.

Jossey-Bass/Pfeiffer

Top Dog

- -

● PURPOSE

- To list items that match certain criteria.

- To identify the most important or most common items in a group.

● SUPPLIES

- An overhead transparency or newsprint flip chart page of the Player Instructions for Top Dog, prepared in advance by the facilitator.

- An overhead projector (if using transparencies) or a newsprint flip chart and felt-tipped markers.

- A set of topics, prepared in advance by the facilitator. (*Note:* These topics should refer to a list that can be ranked in terms of importance, size, frequency, etc.)

- Paper and pencils for the participants.

● STEPS

1. Divide the group into teams of three to five players each.

2. Define the task: "I will name a topic that involves a list of items. Your team has one minute to identify an item from that list. If you correctly identify an item from the list, you will receive 1 point. If you identify the most highly rated item, you will also receive a bonus of 5 points. If the item is not on the list, you receive 0 points."

3. Display the Player Instructions for Top Dog, and name the first topic.

4. After one minute, call time. Have each team name the item it selected. If the item is on the list, the team receives 1 point. If the item is the one rated highest on the list, the team receives its 1 point, plus a bonus of 5 points.

5. Continue for as many rounds as desired.

● SAMPLE PLAY

During a sales and marketing workshop, teams are asked to list as many of the top-ten best-selling U.S. magazines as they can in one minute. After time is called, the facilitator awards the following points for the first team's magazines:

National Geographic @#5	= 1 point
Family Circle @#9	= 1 point
Reader's Digest @#3	= 1 point
Time @#13	= 0 points
Newsweek @#19	= 0 points
Modern Maturity @#2	= 1 point
Odyssey @#1	= 6 points (1 point + 5 bonus points)
Better Homes & Gardens @#6	= 1 point
Total	= 11 points

● CUSTOMIZING TOP DOG

Regarding Group Size

- Use as many teams as necessary to allow maximum participation from each individual (usually no more than five team members).

Regarding Time

- Vary the number of rounds, depending on the time available.

- Allow more or less time per round, depending on the difficulty of the topic.

Regarding the Focus of the Task

- Give each team a list of ten items and have them rank them from #1 to #10. Award points for each correct placement as follows: one point each for the six through ten items, two points each for the two through five items, and five points for the number one item.

- Ask the participants to name any three items on the list and to list them in rank order.

- Have the teams predict the number of points they will score in a specified number of rounds in a particular subject area.

Regarding Scoring

- Award points based on where the item named occurs on the list (e.g., with a five-item list, award 5 points for the #1 item, 4 points for the #2 item, and so on).

PLAYER INSTRUCTIONS FOR
Top Dog

- **Work with your team to name one item on the requested list.**

- **If the item is on the list, score 1 point.**

- **If the item is #1 on the list, score 5 bonus points.**

- **If the item is not on the list, score 0 points.**

● PART THREE ●

● ●

Index

● ●

Finding the Right Game

All of the games described in *Games That Teach* can be adapted to fit a variety of situations. To help in selecting the right game for a specific application, the following section lists certain categories in which particular games work especially well.

The categories in this section are as follows:

- To use with teams with five or fewer players

- To use with teams with five to ten members

- To use with teams with more than ten members

- To use with individuals

- To use as an icebreaker or energizer

- To use creativity and problem-solving skills

- To practice negotiation

- To use with open-ended questions

- To use strategic thinking

- To practice teamwork

- To encourage taking risks

- To present new content information

- To review vocabulary or technical terms

- To recognize relationships among items

- To reward teams for choosing to answer more difficult questions

- To allow teams to challenge one another

To use with teams with five or fewer players:

To use with teams with five to ten members:

To practice negotiation:

To use with open-ended questions:

To use strategic thinking:

To practice teamwork:

To encourage taking risks:

To present new content information:

To review vocabulary or technical terms:

To recognize relationships among items:

To reward teams for choosing to answer more difficult questions:

To allow teams to challenge one another: